JJ THE CPA HERE:

CRACKING THE CPA CODE

I am a CPA.
I know my kind.
I know our CPA code.
And I am going to crack it for you!

This will allow you to achieve more success
in whatever the CPA is holding you back from.

This will allow you to outperform your peers and
competitors.

This will allow you to easily help your clients.

The gate to the next level of success will be open.

All you have to do is unlock one relationship
with one CPA.

And once you CRACK THE CPA CODE with one CPA,
you will be able to crack it with all of them.

Ready?

Are you sure, because with great power comes great
responsibility!

And that i   oking for.
How you har   h their client.

D1402325

I would like to dedicate this book to

my daughter,
Chloe Jenson,
for being the first to believe in JJ the CPA,

my son who has joined the family tradition,
Cooper Jenson,
the future CJ the CPA,

my soulmate
THE AMANDA,
for her loving dedication to JJ the CPA,
being my RODG in everything,
and making this all a reality,

my late Grandad,
Omar Abbott Slayter, CPA,

And my great friend and mentor,
Mark Burson.

Jason O, Jerry K, Tim H, Jason C & Lance B,
thanks for CRACKING MY CPA CODE!

I want to thank those that believed in this book,
promoting it up to 2 years ago when I formed the idea:
Justin McAuliffe, CPA,
Juan Garcia, Jr., THE MARKETER
Jose Zavala
Russell McDonald

And many thanks to my YouTube subscribers,
who believe in JJ the CPA!

TABLE OF CONTENTS

TRUE OR FALSE?

If you learn to CRACK THE CPA CODE, and gain a working relationship with a CPA (able to safely refer your clients and receive referrals) then you can gain a working relationship with anyone?

TRUE!

The CPA is the hardest nut to crack! Through this process of CRACKING THE CPA CODE, you will not only learn how to successfully do business with one of the most revered professionals in the business world, you will be become a magnet to other professionals you wish to do business with because.... You being trusted by the CPA... leads to you being seen as a trusted adviser as well.

How? Why?

Let's think on this. You being trusted by a CPA, sends the *flare-up* to all your allies, competitors and peers, you are someone who is trustworthy!

Question: What does anyone need <u>in you</u>, to refer their clients <u>to you</u>?

My Grandad told me this. *<u>They need to trust you!</u>* Before anything else, someone needs to trust that you are going to take care of, and not take advantage of, their client.

Having a strong, working relationship with the CPA, puts you on the battleship with the CPA, where only trusted advisers are invited on-board.

Therefore, this process of CRACKING THE CPA CODE is not just about gaining one referral source that can take you to the next level of your career. It is about building the foundation of being THE referral source for all those you work with!

If you can climb Mount Kilimanjaro, you can conquer any mountain!

THE SECRET

There are really no secrets once you learn the combination to crack the code to any secret. However, I will give away the one secret that most anyone can relate to, when attempting to work *with* the CPA.

The secret to working with the CPA is to interact with this professional like you would when interacting with your grandparents. Regardless of the CPA's age, communicate with the CPA, like you would your grandmother or grandfather.

Okay, now you know the secret. *Let's get to CRACKING THE CPA CODE!*

WAIT! A WARNING!

You are going to be dealing with one of the most unique personalities in the business world. The CPA. Therefore, this book is full of sarcasm, but I want you to note why.

Yes, it is to make this an interesting read. However, the real reason is to *condition* you before you actually implement the strategies, lessons, principles, and insights I am going to share with you. It is so you can experience, *in a simulation mode*, what you may encounter in dealing with, and trying to work with, the CPA.

So, hang in there. And remember, <u>for the first time in your career, you are going to be</u> *hearing what the CPA is thinking,* as I am going to be sharing my most inner thoughts with, *and about,* you. (And that is not a sarcastic statement.)

This is a huge advantage for you. Think of this as reading the playbook, the answer key, and directions from the other side of the fence, as though you are on the inside.

Here is an example. *Ready? Are you sure?*

The only reason you are reading this book is because you want to take advantage of the client. You want to sell more than what is necessary to the client, because you are only in it for yourself. You don't really care about the client, because you only care about making more money.

Whoa! Seriously JJ?

Yes, I am serious! This is what the CPA thinks of just about *anyone* who encounters the CPA's client.

Do not take this personally.

Do not take this literally.

<u>You know your motives.</u>

I have thought that of you in the past. I can easily think this now, about you. So even though the CPA thinks this, you need to push through that. *Ignore it, because you know* [you know*] it is not true!*

So, you need to overcome the CPA's sarcasm. You can. Easy. *How?* Because you are already now expecting it. It is easy to dodge anything if you know it is coming. So, expect it. I know you can because you are still reading my book. You just got insulted in this simulation, and you kept reading. *Why?* Because you know what the CPA thinks of you simply is <u>not</u> true.

The CPA is very sarcastic.

Why would I put this light on my own profession? Because it is part of the underlying personality we are *trained to take on.* <u>The CPA is trained to be sarcastic</u>. I will share why later in my book, however, before we get to that, let's think about what comes with sarcasm? ***Truth!***

CPAs are sarcastic because we are from the planet Vulcan, and Vulcan's are incapable of lying. Spock, from *Star Trek,* was a Vulcan. (Actually, I cannot lie, he was half Vulcan and half human.) See there is some fun sarcasm!

Let me get serious for a minute though. CPAs cannot lie. We lose everything by lying. If the CPA wants to maintain the CPA letters behind their name, they cannot lie or mislead, in appearance or in fact, about anything. This isn't a suggestion or recommendation from the CPA profession. It is literally a requirement. It is spelled out in the American Institute of Certified Public Accountants (AICPA) Code of Professional Conduct.

Did you catch that? We literally have a CODE in the CPA profession! It's not just for the clever title of my book.

Question: What might be a manner in which you would communicate something you are uncomfortable with? You are getting ready to say something out loud, that you are uncomfortable with saying? How would that actually sound coming out of your mouth? Well, you might be...

wait for it… sarcastic. So, while we are Vulcan, we are also like Spock, human. Which means, when the CPA is in an uncomfortable situation, the CPA typically turns to *sarcasm* when communicating the matter at hand.

When you ask a question like, "Do you think your loved one is fat?" How do you think someone is going to answer that? Most likely with *sarcasm.*

Therefore, because the CPA cannot lie, if we have to answer your question with a "truth" we don't think you or our client will like, it most likely will be accompanied with *sarcasm.*

So, don't be short-sighted. Learn from what the CPA communicates to you, especially when delivered *sarcastically.*

So, if you hear *sarcasm*, you heard some truth. And most likely about you, and/or your product or service. A short-sighted professional would just be insulted and try to beat the CPA. *Not smart.* First, because you will lose. Second, because **when the CPA spits *sarcasm* your way, learn from it**. LEARN FROM IT! PICK IT APART! WE JUST GAVE YOU A HUGE HINT HOW YOU CAN CONVINCE US OTHERWISE.

The CPA's sarcasm is showing you their hand (like in a game of cards).

Sarcasm allows you to see what truth the CPA thinks they believe.

Sarcasm will allow you to better know from the CPA <u>who</u> is at risk, <u>what</u> the concern is, <u>where</u> they are in the process, <u>when</u> they think it should occur, <u>why</u> they don't like it and <u>how</u> they think it should proceed.

What an advantage you now have!

You are going in expecting, and now wanting, to hear the CPA's *sarcasm*, so that you can learn from it. Easy!

Interpret the CPA's *sarcasm* as the CODE to crack with the CPA with a particular situation.

However, now get ready to crack the CPA's CODE overall, to gain a working relationship with the CPA.

THE CODE TO CRACK

As a CPA, here is the BIGGEST thing I think about you, when I get wind you want to do business with my client:

I can't trust you.

That is the CODE, the actual CODE, you need to crack with the CPA! *That you can be trusted!*

Now that you know this, you already have the advantage. *Right? Follow?*

If you go into any situation already knowing what your opponent thinks of you, doesn't that give you a huge advantage? *Of course, it does!*

Before you step into a meeting, if you already knew what your opponent was thinking, you would have a huge advantage going into *that* meeting because you would also know what you think about the situation now as a whole.

"My opponent thinks I am thief, but I know I am not."

"My opponent thinks I can't be trusted, but I know I can."

"My opponent thinks I am only in it for myself, but I know I am in it for my client (too)."

"My opponent thinks they already know *all* about the service or product I am selling, but I know they can't because they don't sell it."

The CPA. Your opponent. Is already thinking, first and foremost, they can't trust you. *Believe it. Get real with it.*

Next, be on alert for the sarcasm, so you know the CODE to crack in that particular situation.

Now, this book isn't about closing <u>one</u> deal. It's about building a long-lasting, working relationship with the CPA. To accomplish that, you have to not just crack the CODE of the "sale," you need to crack the CODE of the CPA… so you can crack the CODE to any situation with the CPA.

Let's get to it, shall we!

THE RULE OF ENGAGMENT

In combat, because that is what you are getting ready to engage in, there are rules. With dealing with the CPA, i.e. engaging with them, <u>there is only one rule</u>.

The client. Is Always. The CPA's client.

Therefore, when you forget this one rule, and you will, I promise you, retreat all actions and communications back to this one rule.

You will know you forgot this one rule because you will walk out of a meeting or hang up the phone with the CPA, or read an email from the CPA and you will be totally perplexed, rubbing your temples, wide-eyed, shaking your head, frustrated and possibly insulted, wondering where all the trust went, that you thought you built up. And this very well may be with the client you referred to the CPA. *Then you will remember, you forgot the*

ONE RULE OF ENGAGEMENT.

The client. Is Always. The CPAs client.

Why is the client never your client? Or why is it that the client is never your client *first?* BECAUSE WE CAN'T TRUST YOU! It's the CODE you need to crack. I just told you this in the last chapter. *Keep up!* (Sarcasm)

I digress. You may be saying to yourself already… "Okay, I will remember that when I am working with the CPA's client. I will always remember they are the CPA's client."

AND YOU WILL FIND YOURSELF IN FAIL MODE
ALREADY.

No matter whose client it is first.
It is always the CPA's client.

You may have worked with your client for the last 20
years, and referred them to the CPA. But you must
remember THE RULE OF ENGAGEMENT.

That client, whose wedding you were in, whose kid you
coached, whose spouse you bought vitamins from for the
last 5 years, and bailed out of jail... You guessed it! They
are no longer your client **[first]** when you are dealing with
the CPA.

That is madness! No way am I doing this JJ. I am out!

And that is where the CPA just won.

If you can't, won't, don't believe the client is always the CPA's clients first, you just lost before you even picked up the "paddle lock" because there is no way you will crack the code!

Good. See we don't need you. Glad you see that you are simply there for yourself, and not your client. You want the ego and control of your client. *How dare you?* As the CPA, we know what is best for the client because we have integrity and objectivity, as stated in the AICPA's CODE. We don't [most of the time] do anything for a commission, so our motives are pure. And you just proved yours motives are not.

Wow!

You are probably thinking, "I am out. No way am I bowing down to the CPA. If I bring a client to a CPA, they are my client first."

You should hope. You should pray, that all your competitors who picked up my book think the same, because that proves my point. When you get to the end of your rope, and you revert back to this one rule of engagement, to stay in the game, you will at some point be the <u>only</u> competitor left standing with that CPA. And you, and you alone, will reap all the rewards. You will be skiing behind your yacht that docks on your other yacht, that you just landed on with your helicopter, because that is your potential of success when you achieve a great working relationship with the CPA. You will have mastered the art of *how to work "with" the CPA.*

So, take a deep breath. Swallow your pride. And let's push on.

Just don't ever, ever, ever, ever, ever, ever, ever forget when dealing with the CPA, the client is the CPA's client first. Then, act accordingly.

LET'S JUST SAY IT!

CPAs are arrogant, insensitive, number crunching, pocket protecting, hard-nosed professionals.

No problem! I got the secret CPA combination to get past that.

But guess what? You need us. You need the CPA. You need the CPA to *like you*. And we know it!

I can turn the tide because I am giving you the combination that the CPA will see... *they need you too.*

And here's the worst part. CPAs are everywhere! Every client you are working with has a CPA involved with them. You can't avoid the CPA; not for long at least.

Good news! I will show you how to make all CPAs your allies.

And just when you think you have the deal done. Signed. Sealed. And delivered. The CPA, with just one word (no), burns it all to the ground.

You are getting ready to learn how to crack that CPA's "no" into the CPA's coveted "yes."

Why do you need us so badly? Because without the CPAs stamp of approval, your client or prospect won't do anything, won't sign anything or hand you *their* yes.

The sequence to cracking the CPA code will be revealed so that the CPA will actually sell the client <u>for you</u>.

So, what is the combination to crack the CPA code?

(Dramatic page turn coming.)

THE COMBINATION TO

CRACKING THE CPA CODE

WWWWWH

A-B-C

1-2-3

10,000,000

100 + 100

30-20-10-3-1-3-10-20-30

COMPLETE <u>YOUR</u> COMBINATION

TO THE CODE WITH <u>EACH</u> CPA HERE

_____

_____

_____

_____

_____

START WITH YOUR TRUST

IN AT LEAST ONE CPA... JJ THE CPA

See if you agree.

The best person to show you how to crack any code would be the one that created the code in the first place. *Right? Makes sense?*

And wouldn't that person even be better equipped to help you master how to crack the code if they also learned how to crack their same code, from the other side of the lock. *You better believe it!*

With that being said, I want you start to gain trust in this process, and to do that, you must first trust at least one CPA. **That will be me**. Even if you have a CPA you work with, either as your own, or with other clients, the trust you need to have in this process may be shaken, especially as we get further in my book. *But I want you to know that I will not let you down.* I will take you to the promise land, and by fully trusting one CPA (JJ the CPA), you will see you can trust all (well most) CPAs.

So, while each CPA is different, the *process* of earning the right to put those 3 letters behind one's name is the same for all CPAs. That process includes <u>one</u> code of ethics for CPAs, <u>one</u> code of conduct for CPAs and <u>one</u> overseeing association for all CPAs. Therefore, there is a common combination to unlock the CPA code, and with me as your master locksmith, from the inside (and out), you need to get ready for a pretty serious uptick in your success in working with the CPA, as it will yield massive results for your top line.

When I say there is one code, I mean there is one code. It is not an opinion or a suggestion. It is a standard set by the overseeing body of the American Institute of CPAs (AICPA).

Guess what? You have access to these codes. These standards. It is public information. If you know the standards, then you know the foundation of the process, or more the expectations, once the process of becoming a CPA is complete.

I have provided a link to these codes on my website. Go to **www.jjthecpa.com** and click on the icon that looks like the cover of this book.

CPAs do NOT have a choice if they want to follow these standards. They are literally set in stone, and the requirement, not just an expectation, is the standards be followed. And if they are not followed and adhered to, the CPA loses everything, as in those 3 letters. *We risk it all.*

I want you to consider this in your own profession. What risks are there for you. Would you lose your credentials? Your identity? The professional achievements of near all achievements in your career?

See when a CPA becomes a CPA, it is taking on an identity that follows the CPA no matter where they go, or what they do. Do you have such credentials that creates such an identity? If you do, you can relate to the CPA. However, most do not have such a risk and so it is difficult for them to understand what is at stake for the CPA, when the CPA is involved.

You may lose the sale. You may lose your job. But unless you do something illegal, you would rebound from that. Recover and move to the next opportunity. The CPA does not have, what we could call, the luxury of just losing the sale, or their job. If a CPA loses their 3 letters, there is no rebounding from it. There is no recovery. It is lost. Forever. It is an identity lost.

Take a minute and digest this.

<u>What would happen if you lost your identity?</u>

Now. What would you do to protect it? To protect your identity, what lengths would you go to?

Who would you trust?   What would allow you to trust someone involved <u>with</u> your business, <u>in</u> your business or with the clients that <u>make up</u> your business?

This is how deep the protection goes for the CPA.

IT TAKES FAITH

Yes, cracking the CPA code is possible.

It takes courage.

It takes persistence. Patience. Perseverance.

It takes faith.

Boom. I am here to tell you, I even had to crack the CPA code, and I am a CPA. It only took me 23 years to do it, but I am letting you practically steal it from me in my book. So, I am going to help you have the courage, persistence, patience, perseverance and *faith*.

You may be wondering, "why all the build-up... to the actual code cracking?" Because without *faith*, you will accomplish nothing. The code you are going to crack with that one CPA is going to take time, and you will be tempted to give up, trash the whole process and yes, lose the *faith*. But don't. You can't. It will be so worth it. That one CPA is going to be your biggest advocate once you reach the level the CPA requires you to reach. You will gain a beautiful professional relationship.

I promise you! *It is worth it!*

You will not only be enriched with wealth, but with an ally that will catch your back. See, we actually need you. There are not many of you that gain our trust. We just need you to be as good as we believe we are… to maintain our reputation… and protect all we have worked for. You will be a part of our tribe. Our crew. Our gang. Our family.

Believe me. You want this. *Keep the faith!*

Talk about *faith*. I have been in the CPA industry for over 27 years and have had my own CPA practice for over 23 years. With that experience I have had someone just like you sitting across from me, and I hated you! But there are those that cracked my CPA code by keeping the *faith*, and it has prospered into the greatest of friendships with massive referrals back and forth over the years.

When I celebrated my 20-year anniversary of my CPA practice, I had huge celebration with my friends, most of which are clients and associates. With five associates in particular, I took the time before the party and estimated the amount of business I had received over those 20 years, and the amount of business I sent them. Easily, with referrals and referrals that lead to referrals, especially those foundational referrals, I had received from each one well over $1 million dollars in fees thus far. And each had (and they agreed) received over $1 million dollars in fees from my referrals. And we are all great friends to boot!

Why?

Because they kept the faith.

This *faith* I speak of. I have had to have it too.

I have a second business that requires I work with other CPAs. Once I unlocked the CPA code (mine) and put it to work on this second business, the referrals started to flow; back and forth.

Not impressed. Let me lay this on you. My second business is selling life insurance. *Yes, I am a life insurance salesman.* You heard right. I got into the perceived sleazy life insurance industry (sarcastic). But check this out: In my first year I became a top 10 [new]

insurance agent in the entire United States with one of the

largest insurance companies in the world. And I did it part-

time with my eyes closed and one hand tied behind my

back (sarcastic) because I put my own principles into

action. And don't think for a minute being a CPA lead to

any initial or immediate trust of me with other CPAs.

Quite the opposite. I lost trust. I was immediately met

with sarcasm and professional skepticism. I had to force

myself to remember I was working with the CPA's client,

and I had to *keep the faith*.

It worked. It works.

BE CONFIDENT IN YOURSELF

You may be asking, "do you think anyone can actually CRACK THE CPA CODE?"

I hear you. You've been beat down by the CPA. Well, guess what? The answer is yes.

And know what else? You will be THE ONE. You are going to CRACK THE CPA CODE my friend.

I have a question for you, before we dig in.

Do you consider yourself successful in business?

I knew it! The answer is yes! You are very successful! That is why you are reading my book. Not only are you successful, but you are one of the best looking professionals any CPA could be lucky enough to do business with.

Here's my point. If you are successful in business, then surely, no doubt about it, you have "tried" to do business with a CPA! And you have cursed the experience, haven't you? *Yes? Yes!*

So, to beat out all of your peers and every competitor, if you want to become a master locksmith when it comes to dealing with the CPA code, **you have to be relentless in your pursuit**. You can't give up. You can't say, well I tried it, and it didn't work, so I am done with CPAs.

Guess why you cannot do that? Because everyone else does. Think of how many will be on the other side of this door when you get there. *Hint: Not many!*

Tell me why you will not do that? The first answer you gave me. Because you consider yourself (correctly) a successful business-person; and that includes, not giving up. I BELIEVE IN YOU MY FRIEND!

You have to give yourself, and that one CPA, that chance.

Listen, if you sucked at business, you would NOT have picked up my book, to see what code needs to be cracked with a CPA.

YOU ARE A SUCCESSFUL, BUSINESS-PERSON.

Don't let the CPA tell you otherwise. Be confident in yourself. We aren't going to make this easy for you, because we want you to show us your confidence. Not arrogance. Confidence.

Alright. So, did I pump you up? Do you feel puffed up? Feeling invincible? Ready to do battle with the CPA?

WRONG! *Never feel that way with a CPA.*

You get puffed up and I will boot you out of my client's life so fast you'll think you are back in 7th grade getting stuffed into a gym locker.

If you think you are invincible, *over me, the CPA*, I will go out of my way to prove to my client you are anything but invincible.

You really think you can go to battle with me? The CPA for my client. I won't sleep until I win, and with one nod of disapproval to my client, you will find yourself tapping out of the wrestling match.

Whoa!?

Wow, JJ, you really had me going there.

I did, didn't I. Maybe.

But guess what? You just started unlocking the code. I just told you what I am thinking when you come at me acting invincible; like more than half of you come at me.

Boom! You keep going and you will have already beaten out half your peers and competitors in working with the CPA. *Nicely done! Now stay with me...*

WHAT IS THE KEY

You ever seen the type of lock that has both a combination on the front (the thing your turn left and right with all the numbers) AND a keyhole in the back? This is no different.

Yes, there is a combination to the CPA CODE, but there is also a key.

The key to CRACKING THE CPA CODE is to learn how to work "with" the client. Key word "with."

So, once you know how to do this, and successfully, you will be able to use that same key with other CPAs.

You may be tempted (like so many of your predecessors) to just find *some* key factor you *think* works for you, but I promise you the key can only be revealed once you learn the combination. The reason for this is that <u>YOU are a key part of the combination.</u>

It will take time for you to discover how you best work "with" the CPA. That's right, you have a something at stake here too. Your reputation, starting with your reputation with your client(s) whom you introduce to the CPA. You need to feel comfortable with the process and not just give into the CPA, and their demands alone. So, when you figure out the combination to CRACKING THE CPA code, you will then also solve the easier side of this, because you will have the key. And what is the key? You! <u>You are the key</u>, and you will have defined for yourself how you want to fit your clients into a CPAs practice and vice-versa.

Now I want you to note that not every key fits every lock, but it is true there are master keys that can fit most. *Right?* So, <u>you</u> will be that master-locksmith with such a key.

Later in my book I will walk you through step-by-step how to narrow down the locks (the CPAs) to *that one CPA that lead you to the promise land.*

Here's a hint to that combination:

30-20-10-3-1-3-10-20-30

WHY IS THERE A CODE TO CRACK?

Why is there even a code to crack with the CPA? Well, to be blunt, while we don't think you are a low down, sleezy salesperson, we see most of you (that want to do business with our clients) as a necessary evil, that we must tolerate. (*I told you there would be sarcasm.*)

Okay. Let's get serious.

THE REASON THERE IS A CODE TO CRACK IS *WE DON'T TRUST YOU.*

I am being dead serious. We are actually trained not trust you. In fact, <u>we are trained not to even trust our own client.</u> (No wonder the divorce rate amongst CPAs is higher than the national average.) But it's true.

Maybe this makes you feel better about the whole situation of working with CPAs in that they literally don't even trust their *own* clients.

Now let me qualify that. We trust our clients, otherwise we wouldn't allow them to be our clients. But we have been trained to constantly evaluate (and re-evaluate) if we can continue to trust our clients, based on their actions, needs, wants, requests, and who they involve themselves with (you being one of those factors).

So, when you enter the relationship between the client and the CPA, you instantly and automatically cause the CPA to re-evaluate everything. Again, because we are trained to.

Secondly, possibly sarcastically, we don't trust our clients *with you*. Let me also qualify that. We don't trust our clients to know better than to be fooled by you. And when I say fooled, I mean sold, by you. This more politely is that we want to protect our clients from you, because our clients may not know any better, and in essence we are concerned that our client can't be trusted to make the best decision for themselves, with your influence on the matter.

Where does this distrust come from? Why is it so prevalent amongst CPAs? Again, because we were trained to be *professionally skeptical.* A term literally used in the CPA world, from the college classroom to the CPA exam to the AICPA standard is the term (and understanding the definition of) *professional skepticism.*

I recall in college, my professor spending a lot of time and effort explaining what *professional skepticism* is, why we are required to use it and how to implement it. That was in the auditing course, which by the way, is a required course for all accounting students, to obtain their accounting degree. And, check this out, it is a huge part of the CPA exam and is inherent to the AICPA standards.

The AICPA has a course titled, *Professional Skepticism: The Art and Science of Being Columbo*. The description is: "Professional skepticism is an attitude that includes a questioning mind, being alert to conditions which may indicate possible misstatement due to error or fraud, and a critical assessment of audit evidence." NOTE: This description wasn't made up by a clever author. It is literally from (word for word) from the section entitled *Professional Skepticism* in the AICPA's standards of *Due Professional Care in the Performance of Work.*

Therefore, CPAs spend a lot of time learning how to implement *professional skepticism*. <u>Stated another way, we are trained not to trust you or our clients.</u> If I was being sarcastic… you might say we are brainwashed into this thinking. Believe me, it is a blessing and a curse. But I will tell you one thing, *professional skepticism* has saved me and my clients many, many times from the horror stories you read about in the Wall Street Journal that many other professionals may not have picked up on; or at least not early enough. Why? Because other professions aren't trained on how to NOT trust others.

Seriously. Think about that line of thinking. As humans, we are inherently trusting, and value trustworthiness. CPAs are trained to be trustworthy, but to constantly question the trustworthiness of others.

Now knowing CPAs are trained to *not* trust YOU, not only should this make you feel better, but it should be warming you up to the idea that you can and will CRACK THE CPA CODE because you are getting this inside look.

START AT PROFESSIONAL SKEPTICISM

Let's continue with our discussion on *professional skepticism* because <u>if you know when this is exercised by the CPA, then you will know when to be prepared for it.</u>

Knowing *professional skepticism* is created in the seed of what produces the CPA, you should know that *professional skepticism* <u>is implemented from the get-go.</u>

The biggest aspect of implementing *professional skepticism*, based on our training, is you can't wait to exercise it. CPAs must begin the thought process of *professional skepticism* before anything actually happens. Therefore, keep this in mind, before you actually start anything with the CPA's client (remember THE RULE OF ENGAGEMENT). You need and must remember the clock has already started ticking in the CPAs mind on how long they will tolerate you proceeding with your "sale."

Ever seen the movie The Godfather? Or any gangster movie for that matter? Think of the CPA as the Godfather or the Godmother. What is always crucial with "The Boss?" That you pay your respects, and more importantly, you ask for permission. And what happens when you don't ask for permission? Worse yet, let me state this another way... What happens when someone has to ask for forgiveness from the Godfather or Godmother? Hint: It involves "sleeping with the fishes."

Pay your respects. Ask for permission.

If you think about it, why does "The Boss" expect and require this. Dig deep... Because the Godfather, the

Godmother is *professionally skeptical*? Am I right? Who do you think came up with... "Keep your friends close, and your enemies closer." That is the result of *professional skepticism*.

Back to the CPA's training, it is so detailed that it seems we (me included) have a sonar radar that detects you, even before you breath in the CPA's direction.

I know you are on the hunt for my client well before you think I do. *How? Hello!* Because... the client (our client, my client) has already told me something about you, their consideration and/or need for whatever it is you are selling them.

Capeesh?

By paying your respects, and asking for permission, this will prove you have good intentions with the CPA's client, and you have nothing to hide. It also allows the CPA to express their concerns, wants and expectations for *how this will go down.*

Now, you may be asking, *how many times do I need to pay my respects and ask for permission?* <u>As many times as it takes.</u>

Two notes here:

1. After doing this as many times as it takes with the CPA, you will at some point NOT have to do this, at least not in the same cautious manner. <u>As long as what you are doing has not deviated from the past process,</u> the CPA will grow to trust you. At least

with that one aspect, as you move forward. And when this happens, you are on your way.

2. The loyalty you show the CPA, at some point (not as fast as you'd hope) will share in that loyalty with you. And the CPA is very loyal: *once it's deserved.*

THE CODE CRACKING COMBINATION

W

W

W

W

W

H

WHO

WHAT

WHERE

WHEN

WHY

HOW

This is the code cracking combination that you should apply to each [and every] situation where you are going to work "with" the CPA. This should be easy to remember since we *should have* all learned this in grade school.

W W W W W H

Who? What? Where? When? Why? and How?

Any good, successful story (sale), needs to have the 5 W's and 1 H. Go through this exercise with each sale so you will be prepared when the CPA asks you...

Who are you?

What is the service/product?

Where are you doing this?

When are you doing this?

Why (in the world) are you doing this?

and

How do you plan to do this (and pull this off)?

If you don't have these basic answers ready for the CPA, you simply won't get the deal done; *or least not like you hoped.* Whatever question you don't have a good answer for, well, it will be just like when your teacher graded your paper (sale). So, do you want an A, B or C?

A B C

The CPA actual code you need to crack is... how to work "with" one CPA. The whole goal here is to unlock one great CPA relationship because it only takes one to gain millions of dollars in referrals.

Let's go to the basics. A B C.

Now if you know me already, you would be thinking I would be going into…

A – Always

B- Be

C-Closing.

Normally I would, but we are talking about CRACKING THE CPA CODE, and we would be exercising massive *professional skepticism* with that approach. **See… you are learning!**

Nope. I am talking about the ABCs of our kind, and by our kind, I mean the CPA.

We are

    Awkward, Arrogant Advocates *that*

    Believe Bigger is not Better, *and*

    Clients Can't Control *themselves.*

You probably just see us as…

    Average **B**ean **C**ounters.

Am I right?

So, maddening isn't it? The freaking *average bean counting* CPA.

CPAs never return phone calls!
Won't take the time to reply, or at least not timely!

These CPAs treat you like a "salesperson," whether you are a lawyer, financial advisor, insurance professional, IT expert, software consultant or even a CPA yourself! Sheesh!

Who do these CPAs think they are?!

I will tell you, they are <u>the CPA</u>, and they hold all the cards.

The CPA has your client or prospect locked up. They protect the gate, seeing you as the fox wanting into the hen house; with only one intent… *to negatively affect their client.*

YOU WANT REFERRALS?

Let's go to the next part of working "with" the CPA: referrals. You want referrals from the CPA? *Ummm, of course you do!* When does that happen? *Never. Right?* Well that is all about to change!

I travel around the United States teaching tax courses, and the number one complaint I hear about CPAs is… "they never refer!" Second complaint is, "the CPA doesn't care about my referrals."

I mean, heaven forbid, you would want to refer your client or prospect to the CPA? The CPA will say, *"Sorry, full!"* You know I am right here. Heck, I am that CPA right now.

Ever *dared* to work "with" your own client while involving their CPA? Of course, you have! You wouldn't be reading this book if you hadn't.

At a seminar in Chicago, I asked group of massively successful insurance and investment professionals about their experiences with doing business with the CPA. Here's what I heard:

"Why are CPAs so awkwardly arrogant?"

"Why is it so hard to do business with a CPA?"

"Why do CPAs seem to crush your hopes and dreams, right in front of your client?"

"Why would a CPA take your well crafted, extremely thought out plan and obliterated in 30 seconds flat?"

"Why the heck does a CPA think they know it all? And actually think they know my business better than me?"

"CPAs are super smart, but super arrogant in the weirdest way."

Here's the interesting part, and well, very sad. Did you note what I asked this group. I simply asked about their <u>experience</u> in working with CPAs. I didn't ask about the struggles or challenges of working with CPAs; or even what they hate about working with CPAs. The only responses I got, were the ones I just shared with you. *All of them being negative.* **So, don't feel alone!** <u>You aren't.</u>

But you will be the one that conquers this because that all is going to change. Now! Soon the CPA will love you!

Back to the A B C's of the CPA:

Awkward, arrogant advocates that believe bigger is not better, and clients can't control themselves.

Don't see us as average bean counters. Don't just pretend you don't. Do not.

So how do you work with a CPA, now knowing their ABCs? The answer. Very carefully.

In all seriousness, you may be saying the same things on the aforementioned experiences. I get it. *I really do.* I have even said the same things when trying to help my prospects with their life insurance needs who were with other CPAs.

Let's break this down!

<u>Why is the CPA perceived as awkward?</u> Most of the time it is because we make decisions based on facts, and not emotion; i.e. Spock. Therefore, be factual in your approach; not emotional. You wouldn't say, *do you feel the client needs this service or product?* You would say, the client needs this service or product because _____ (insert the facts).

<u>Why are CPAs arrogant?</u> Well, for starters, we worked harder to get where we are because we not only had to get a college degree, but had to pass one of the hardest exams in the world as well as work under the supervision of

another CPA for two years to get where we are at. Not to mention we are required to take 40 hours of continuing education *each* year, including 2 hours of ethics. Clearly you are inferior and no matter your profession, you don't work as hard as us, nor do you know the responsibilities we carry for our clients.

Okay, okay! Wait. What I am writing here? *I am sharing with you, honestly, what is going through the CPA's head.* I am just laying it out there for you, as blunt as I can be. *Not saying it's true.* Remember, you are getting the hear what the CPA is thinking.

While all those requirements are true, it certainly doesn't make us better than you (maybe), but we have more to risk than you (possibly). Remember if we don't do things properly, we could lose those 3 letters (CPA), and thus, all that hard work and commitment we put in would be ruined. The CPA has a lot (more) to protect; in our minds. The arrogance is a deflector and our first line of defense. We don't mean to be arrogant. *We just don't want you… to cause us… to screw up.*

Don't react to our arrogance by trying to show us you know more or better. React with an approach to find out what the CPA doesn't know; *that they think they know.* Relieve the pressure that you are seeing as arrogance. And those goes back to **WWWWWH**. *Right?*

<u>Why is the CPA such a hard-core advocate?</u> It comes from the second letter in our credentials. P. P for public. We are a Certified *Public* Accountant. We take an oath, literally, to serve the public at large. The public doesn't just necessarily mean our clients. *It means everyone.*

What is bred into the CPA is… you are an advocate for the public. Therefore, the best way to work "with" a CPA is to show how you too are an advocate for your client or prospect. (Sorry, their client.) And how do you do that?

W W W W W H

Why don't we believe bigger is better?

Bigger means it is more than needed. Costs more than needed. So don't come guns a blazing with how whatever you are selling is bigger than everyone else's. We don't necessarily need to know what you are selling is better. *That is selling.* Bells and whistles, along with size and options, doesn't make anything better.

What makes something better, is that it is simply a fit for the client or prospect; regardless how it compares to your competitor or another product. It is either a fit for the client or not. Stick the facts…

W W W W W H

<u>Why do we believe clients can't control themselves?</u>

Because they can't. *Just kidding.*

Let me break it down *real simple like*, as they say in Oklahoma. If a client could control themselves they wouldn't be asking us about it.

However, what is even worse is, if the client *thinks* they can control themselves, and didn't check with us (the

CPA) first, they clearly have proven... they can't control themselves. (Remember the Godfather/Godmother syndrome.)

Here is how it has been proven to us CPAs over and over; that clients can't control themselves. When a client asks us before (or tells us after), we want to know... you guessed it... the WWWWWH, and about 99% of the time, the client can't give us the *whole story*; the WWWWWH. And to boot, they tell us all their emotions related to the story. Therefore, if the client can't tell us the simple WWWWWH, it seems logical (Spock) that the client couldn't or can't control themselves. *Make sense?*

When you tell us the WWWWWH, while we appreciate that, we have to make sure our client understands the WWWWWH. Because if the client can tell us, then we know we won't be held responsible and we can most likely put our *professional skepticism* to rest.

Without the combination of WWWWWH, the CPA code cannot be cracked.

You want to work "with" the CPA, know [up and down] the WWWWWH.

How does the WWWWWH apply to getting referrals?

When working "with" the CPA and providing the WWWWWH of what you are selling, the CPA starts getting comfortable not only with you, but with your WWWWWH. The proof they are warming up to you and what you are selling is... they allow(ed) it to happen. And the more the CPA allows it to happen, the more they actually accept you and believe your WWWWWH.

Eventually the CPA will see (*without you ever, ever, ever pointing this out to the CPA*) ...

Who of their clients could benefit from this?

What clients of theirs does this also apply to?

Where are their clients in need of this?

When are their clients ready for this?

Why their clients should have this?

How their clients can get this.

Bingo! Referrals start flying your way!

See, once the CPA can wrap their logical thinking around your WWWWWH, apply their *professional skepticism* to your WWWWWH, and know you will be around to see the WWWWWH through, the CPA will actually become an advocate for you and what you are selling. And, once the CPA sees that the client actually bought whatever it is that you are selling, the benefits, and that it didn't implode, the CPA will want their other clients to benefit the same. *Why?* Because CPAs are extremely fair (objective), and we wouldn't want one client to benefit more than another from something we were aware of… and didn't share.

Let me say this another way, while you really let this sink in. The CPA wants each of their clients to benefit equally from their knowledge. Once your WWWWWH becomes their WWWWWH, they will want all their clients to share in that same knowledge, i.e. your service or product. When this occurs, the flood gates open with referrals to you.

Hold up! Wait a second! Before your mind starts blowing into what the promise land looks like, know this. As soon as your WWWWWH changes, you must circle back to the

CPA, pay your respects and get permission. *Pretty easy, but you still must do it. And do NOT forget!*

Let me really reiterate this.

When your WWWWWH becomes the CPA's WWWWWH, by you changing one of the W's or the How, this changes the CPAs perspective of ALL the WWWWWH's and enters *professional skepticism.* So, what do you do to ensure the CPA understands what changed? You guessed it. Pay your respects, and ask for their permission.

Let me beat this into your way of thinking. Like really put this at the foundation of ensuring you continue to get *piles* of referrals from the CPA.

At the drop of a hat, the CPA can go back to not trusting you! DO NOT EVER FORGET THAT. *The CPA trusts you with your WWWWWH.* They don't trust you, and you alone. The CPA trusts you *AND* your WWWWWH.

Stated another way. The CPA that trusts your WWWWWH, trusts you to implement the same WWWWWH. The CPA doesn't *really* trust you to do anything different with their client (RULE OF ENGAGEMENT).

Follow? Good! *You are getting good at this my friend!*

Bottom line: Know your WWWWWH and apply it to the A-B-C's of the CPA.

1-2-3: CRACKING TO CLOSE

You've got your WWWWWH and know the A-B-C's of the CPA, but how do you close the deal with the CPA?

It is as simple as 1-2-3.

Now I am not saying 1-2-3 to be cute. I mean KISS! "Keep it simple, stupid!" The U.S. Navy coined this back in 1960 as a design principle.

The KISS principle states that *"most systems work best if they are kept simple rather than made complicated; therefore, simplicity should be a key goal in design, and unnecessary complexity should be avoided."* (FYI -This has been associated with aircraft engineer Kelly Johnson.)

Therefore, once you've established the WWWWW, expand your H (how) into an easy 1-2-3 and apply it to the A-B-C's of the CPA.

KISS is how you will close. As in the most basic of basics of "how" it will be closed.

When you present the "how" to the CPA, it simply means you have a plan of action of "how" this works. You provide the ending.

This isn't a suspense novel you are presenting to the CPA.

Sharing the "how" is sharing the ending to your story. Sharing the "how" allows the CPA to know ahead of time *how this will close* with <u>their client</u>.

Examples to share with the CPA:

Step 1: Complete the application.

Step 2: Wait for approval.

Step 3: Sign life insurance policy.

Step 1: Complete the questionnaire.

Step 2: Make any changes.

Step 3: Sign the Will.

Step 1: Complete the application.

Step 2: Wait for approval.

Step 3: Sign the bank loan documents.

Step 1: Complete the paperwork.

Step 2: Deposit the funds.

Step 3: Pull funds when you retire.

Let me be clear. KISS doesn't then include sub-sections to each step, when presented to the CPA. KISS doesn't require a meeting. KISS doesn't require further selling the product or service. KISS doesn't spell out what happens if the client or prospect doesn't do this. KISS doesn't include a chart, graphs or a pie-chart. And in no way shape or form does KISS include results. DID YOU CATCH THAT? **KISS does NOT include results!**

Here is my point. Make it easy. And it should be easy! If you have solved for who, what, where, when and why with the CPA, then the how is simply the close, and that should be easy, easy. Again, expand the how into a KISS 1-2-3 and you will close (when you are ready to close).

Know what else this accomplishes? When it is time to close, you don't have to go back to the Godfather or Godmother to ask permission to close. Bazinga!

Now, if you have to circle back to any of the W's, by already establishing for the CPA how it closes back at the time you initially paid your respects, you won't have to go over the H again... as long as you made the *how* (the close) simple from the get go.

Don't make the CPA have to solve for the H every time a W changes. By keeping the close simple upon simple, the CPA knows that whatever changed will still lead to the same close.

Know what I am thinking right now? That you will still want to wait to share the *how* with the CPA, because you want to make sure the sale happens, or it is a fit for the client, or it's different from client to client etc. etc. *Are you kidding me right now?* My teeth are gritting right now! Your how, the close, is not contingent on the W's. *Follow?* Go back to my examples. Those 1-2-3 steps are as generic as you can get. KISS! KEEP IT SIMPLE, STUPID.

I will say it again. If your *how* is simple. Your *close* is simple. So just freaking share it up-front. Anything else makes me question you! And worse, when I learn later it closed, and I didn't know *how*, I will go out of my way to unwind your deal. I promise you that!

So, tell us the proverbial ending…

and they lived happily ever after!

You don't need to add…

and they lived happily ever after…

as long as this _____ happens!

No. No! No! No! No!

If you need to add anything, you do it in the WWWWW.

When you equate the *how* to a set of variables, we will <u>not</u> go there with you.

Why?

Because we are NEVER, EVER, EVER, EVER, EVER going to sign-off on your *theoretical* results. We cannot. *Shall not.* <u>Will not</u> give our approval of the results.

Let me make sure we are on the same page. Your client or prospect has a need, and for you to solve for that need you explain how what you are providing will solve the need. That is called a "sale," which most likely evokes emotion. Now, you may still provide your version of "how" to your client or prospect, but that version of "how" to the CPA is a sale.

Really think about this.

You CLOSE the deal BEFORE you actually perform anything. *Right?* KISS!

The "how" to you may be *how* you will perform the services, but the CPA wants to know "how" the deal will close for you to perform those services. KISS!

We are talking about Spock here. Okay.

Remember A-B-C's?

Don't confuse "paying" for the *close*, as the close here. Yes, the close includes payment, but payment does not occur before the *close*. KISS!

The *close* is <u>not</u> your results. You have to *close* before you can even provide results. KISS!

You are not being deceitful with the CPA or providing another version of the "how." You are providing the literal "how" that Spock needs to be aware of. KISS!

Think on this carefully. KISS!

Let's circle back to providing a 1-2-3, KISS "how" when paying your respects to the Godfather, Godmother; I mean the CPA.

When you actually share it up-front, this allows the CPA to give <u>you</u> permission to close the deal.

Be aware that this will also cause them to inquire more at that time, as they will see the close in-sight. *Don't get deterred here.* By having your WWWWW ready, you are able to satisfy the CPA's inquiries on-the-spot. Also remember, the more the CPA inquires, the more you learn. The more the CPA understands *it will close when WWWWW occurs*, the more the CPA will NOT muck things up when you actually close. And if they do try to jump back into the equation after the close, you can easily keep everything in-tact because you can remind them the ending did not change.

Ever said, *"but it didn't change anything."*

When the "how" is NOT the results, the "how" doesn't change.

So, even if you are still working out the life insurance rating, who the contingent beneficiaries are in the Will, the length of the loan or the risk tolerances to invest, the CPA will know, once that is solved, the client will 1-2-3 to close.

If you cover the major strokes of WWWWW and How, the majority of the time the CPA will have seen the full picture. And with that full picture, including the 1-2-3 close, you won't have to start from scratch every time the CPA re-visits the issue BECAUSE they already know "how" you will close the deal. 1-2-3

What I am describing may seem elementary to you; even obvious. But don't get ahead of yourself, not even for one second. You miss this 1-2-3 and guess what we think? *That you were trying to get one past us.* You aren't paying your respects. You aren't asking for permission. Then you will find yourself back peddling, asking for forgiveness, hoping your deal isn't getting ready to go "sleep with the fishes."

Remember what you are trying to accomplish here. You want to have ONE great relationship with ONE CPA.

Without it, there is no way you can be as successful as... you can be! *I'm being serious!*

The CPA is the missing piece to you achieving all of your wildest dreams, because the CPA unlocks every sale you could ever imagine making. 1-2-3

You know the CPA holds all the cards and the sooner you crack the CPA code with one CPA, the quicker you will achieve ultimate success! 1-2-3

You won't find ways to work around the CPA. They don't exist. Am I right? Of course I am or you wouldn't be this far into reading my book right now. 1-2-3

So, are you getting a sense of what the combination is to work with the CPA and crack our code?

ABC

WWWWWH

1-2-3 (KISS)

Believe it or not, most CPAs don't even know any of this about themselves. They think they have their client's secrets all locked up. Well, to most, that very well may be true. However, for you, not so much.

EACH CPA COULD HAVE

A $10 MILLION DOLLAR PRACTICE

Let's get down to brass tax, shall we! Let's talk dollars and cents!

Let me set the stage on how CRACKING THE CPA CODE directly helps you make more money, and get you even more excited about CRACKING THE CPA CODE, because if you aren't already, you need to be.

Ready? Close your eyes and imagine you being as wealthy as you want to be because you finally found a CPA you can trust. *That believes in you.*

Okay. Now. Open your eyes.

See, this is CPA humor. And right now, you should grinnin' ear to ear, baby!

Stay with me.

Think of all of the clients a CPA works with. <u>Seriously.</u>

Take 10 seconds and allow let your imagination run wild. *Okay, that's long enough!* (CPA humor.)

Think of the smallest CPA practice you know, even a solo practitioner working from home, and imagine how many clients they are working with. Pssst: I will share my numbers with my CPA practice with you after you daydream of all the ways you will increase your success rate.

Wait. I get it. You just thought of all the clients the smallest CPA firm has, and you were <u>NOT</u> blown away.

WRONG! You aren't seeing what I am seeing, so let me show you how my practice is literally worth $10,000,000 <u>to you.</u> As in *TEN MILLION DOLLARS*.

Yes!

There we go.

Now I have your attention.

How many clients is not how you should be thinking anyhow.

Think how much each client is worth to you, in fees. Think like this:

Bankers: How many loans does one CPA have with all their clients?

Insurance Professionals: How many lives does one CPA work with?

Investment Advisers: How many investment dollars does one CPA have amongst its clients?

Attorneys: How many Wills, Trusts or new business setups are there with one CPA? How many of their clients will be involved with just one lawsuit, car accident or divorce this year?

IT & Copier Pro's: Count up all the computers the CPA's clients have. Not the computers in the CPAs offices. The number of computers all of their clients use.

Any sales professional selling anything, to anyone: How many of the CPA's clients use or would use what you are selling?

The answer is simple:

More than you can handle!

That's right! Just one relationship with one CPA [or one CPA firm] could generate more work than you can handle in your entire career! Trust me.

So, don't look at this necessarily as how do you do business with CPAs. Look at this as how you will do business with <u>one</u> CPA? Think how easy that is. *Find one CPA that you can refer to and get referrals from, and you will be the envy of everyone around you.*

You want details? Fine. Let's put some dollars to this theory.

As I shared, I have been in the CPA profession for over 27 years and have had my own CPA practice over 23 years (still going strong). I have worked with thousands of clients, and with that, hundreds of *money-hungry salespeople* like you. Yes, you! (That's sarcasm.)

Note this: In the last 3 years I have downsized my practice from 13 people in my firm, down to 4, including me. From over 2,000 tax returns down to the numbers I am going to share with you now. The reason it is important to comprehend this, is that the numbers I am about to share with you are based on my actual, current client list, and I am now a <u>one</u> CPA show.

To make this obvious. This is what ONE CPA can offer.
The basic statistics of my practice as of the publishing of
this book:

587 tax returns.

308 business returns and 279 individual returns.

Of the individual returns, 113 are single and 166 are
married (445 adults in total).

418 claimed dependents.

Of the business returns, there are 1,683 employees in
addition to the owners.

Ready for some real numbers?

Insurance Professionals:

How many lives do I have within my client group?

863 lives, not counting extended family, or adult children.

2,546 lives if you include the employees of the businesses I work with.

Average first year commission (FYC) at an average of $67 per month premium with 45% commission is potentially **$921,143** to your pocket, on life insurance products alone.

Can you even write that many policies in one year?

Bankers:

How many potential loans do I have with all my clients?

279 home mortgages at an average of $300,000 per mortgage is $83,700,000 in potential personal loans.

308 business loans and/or lines of credit at an average of $150,000 per is $46,200,000 in potential business loans.

Not even counting potential car loans or 2nd loans, that is a total potential of 587 loans or $129,900,000.

With a 1% origination fee, that is **$1,299,000** in fees, with the 1st year of interest collected at 4% of **$5,196,000.**

Can your bank even loan that much out?

Investment Advisers:

How many investment dollars do I have amongst my clients?

At an average of $50,000 per adult ($22,250,000), $250,000 per business ($77,000,000) and $5,000 dependent ($2,090,000), that potentially is $101,340,000 in assets.

At 1% management fee that is potentially **$1,013,400** to your top line, in *a single year*.

Can you manage all that alone? You'd need an army.

Attorneys:

How many Wills? (445) $1,500 each: $667,500 in legal fees.

How many Trusts? (279) $550 each: $153,450 in legal fees.

How many new business setups? (308) $1,200 each: $369,600 in legal fees.

How many of my clients will be involved with just one lawsuit each year? (Guessing 3% or 17 annually) At $15,000 each: $255,000 annually in legal fees.

How many car accidents per year? (Guessing .5% or half percent or 3 annually) At $9,000 in net attorney fees for each case: $27,000 annually (if not millions).

How many divorces each year? (Guessing of 166 married couples, 2% or 3 annually) At $15,000 each: $45,000 annually.

For a full-service law firm that is a potential legal fee to the top line of **$1,517,550**. *(And you know my fees are low.)*

How many lawyers would need to have to just handle one CPA's group of clients? (Sounds like the start of an old lawyer joke.)

IT & Copier Pro's:

Count up all the computers just for the adults in my client list, plus half of the kids, that is 654 computers.

654 computer issues to fix.

654 computers to replace.

At $1,000 per computer for replacement, not even counting employees, that is **$654,000**.

Any Sales Professional selling anything, to anyone: How many of my clients need or would buy what you are selling?

You get the picture, but just in life insurance commissions, bank origination fees and interest, money management fees, legal fees and computer costs, my small, one CPA practice (mine) has **$10,601,093** to potentially pay other professionals (most of which could be in just one year).

Go back and add that all up (what I underlined). With 587 tax returns, my practice is worth over $10 million dollars to just those professional groups I mentioned. That doesn't even count whatever you are going to try and sell to my clients.

With just <u>one</u> CPA... $10 million.

Think if you *and I* just did business together. Might be all

you could handle. You'd have to bring on some help, I'd

imagine.

YOU'VE GOT ONE WEEK A MONTH

Here is some good news! There is pretty much one week a month that is best to work with the CPA.

So, this chapter is simple.

The 3rd week is your best bet.

The 3rd week of every month, is your window.

The best week, and the only week, you should try your very best to have any meaningful interaction with the CPA, is the 3rd week.

More to come, but this is HUGE for you to remember.

Why?

Think on it, but I will explain.

I wanted to make this chapter simple because you don't need to really understand why... do you? <u>You just need to work "with" the CPA during the 3rd week.</u>

Want to start a relationship with the CPA? Great. Do it in the 3rd week of the month.

Want to meet with the CPA? Great. In the 3rd week of the month.

Want the CPA to... you guessed it, do it in the 3rd week of the month. <u>Any month.</u>

Even November? Yes.

What about December? Yes.

April? Yes.

"Oooooh, now I get it!"

See during most months, there is some kind of deadline, and pretty much that deadline is on the 15th of the month. You don't want to catch the CPA during the first 2 weeks because they are tied up with the deadline. You want to avoid the last week of the month as they are already working on the next deadline, or secondly, many months also include a deadline at the end of the month.

So. The 3rd week it is!

WORKING "WITH" THE CPA

Let's circle back. How is it that I, JJ THE CPA, know the code? THE CPA CODE! Because you've never met a CPA quite like me! Well, that is a fact, and because I have been on *both* sides of the table. *Right?*

Remember the one and only code we are breaking: How to work *with* the CPA. The key word being "with."

You need to find ways to work *with* the CPA. And with that comes a list, a long list, of Do's and Don'ts while you are working *with* the CPA. I am going to share this list with you, so don't stop here.

Don't get put off reading past here. Keep going!

I am giving you the keys along with the combination with these Do's and Don'ts. Think of these as knowing which way to turn the knob while entering in the combination. Remember the combination lock to your locker, bike or shed? And how hard it was to remember at first?

Left to 30. Right to 20. Back left to 10.

or was it right, left, right?

Read these Do's and Don'ts coming up like a treasure map, with a clear picture of where X marks the spot.

You are having the rare opportunity to get inside the head the CPA, and right now, I am *all* CPAs to you.

Buckle up!

DO's and DON'Ts

DO THIS.

DO NOT DO THIS.

DO. DON'T.

THIS LEADS TO

OPEN SESAME.

Because I think, *you think*, you already have it all figured out I'm going try and buck you off with these do's and don'ts to get you properly situated for how you need to approach, create, build, maintain and flourish with a long lasting relationship with a Certified Public Accountant.

I WANT TO REMIND YOU OF

MY PREFACE,

WHICH WAS A WARNING

Repeating what I stated before: You are going to be dealing with one of the most unique personalities in the business world. The CPA. Therefore, this book is full of sarcasm, but I want you to note why. Yes, it is to make this an interesting read, however, the real reason is to *condition* you before you actually implement the strategies, lessons, principles, and insights I am sharing with you. It is so you can experience, in a simulation mode, what you may encounter in dealing with, and trying to work with, the CPA. So, hang in there. And remember, for the first time in your career, you are hearing what the CPA is thinking. Added note: In the beginning of these Do's and Don'ts I will remind you I am being sarcastic, but after the first few... *practice knowing it.*

DON'T ASK FOR REFERRALS. EVER!

A CPA sees you as an untrustworthy predator that is going to take advantage of their client. *Sorry!*

Crazy right? True. I hated you. Still do. (Sarcasm) I don't care who you are. Don't come along and try to impress me with your slick brochure, free pen, Chester the cat smile and promise of referrals *to me.* I see you a mile away and I know you are just going to sell my client something they don't need or want. I am convinced of it. I may have known you for 20 years, but the second you ask for a referral you are my mortal enemy because I do not trust you. (Sarcasm) The CPA industry is the most trusted profession in the world, second only to the clergy. We have worked hard to earn that trust and even harder to keep it. And so you come along and you might throw a monkey wrench into my client relationship, and I can't have that.

A CPA makes a huge commitment when they agree to work with a client, one they expect to last for decades, and historically has. Because I will be working with my client for years to come, if I refer my client to you, and you do one thing wrong, I will hear about it for many years to come. *Make sense?*

Why is the CPA so distrustful (besides our training)? Because we have already been burned by you (or someone like you); and every one of you are the same. So, don't tell me you are any different. You aren't. (Sarcasm)

You probably won't be around for long either; *is what CPAs think.* I have seen it firsthand. You are in the insurance industry today, and gone tomorrow. You are a financial advisor with a different broker every 2 years. You practice law with a large firm now, but out on your own later. You sell copiers this time, but next time you will be selling projectors. And when the CPA thinks you won't be around, they know they will have to pick up the pieces you left behind, long after you collected your commission or fee.

See, we just can't trust you. So do NOT ask me for a referral.

What do you do then? Wait for the referral? Yes! If you take care of my client(s), and I see that you are going to be here for the long haul (with me as the CPA), I will start to refer to you. *Promise!*

DO ASK FOR ONE PIECE OF ADVICE.

A CPA sees you as a trustworthy teammate that is going to take care of their client if you ask them for advice with one matter.

You don't need any advice, right? *Wrong!*

I can tell you right now, a CPA knows you do not know everything "about *their* client" and so you do need our advice. Notice what we know you don't know everything about. <u>You don't know *my* client, like I do</u>. And remember, once the CPA starts working with the client, even yours, it is the CPAs client first; *remember.*

This is NOT advice about *what you do*. If it was, a CPA will think you are an idiot and they for sure won't send you any referrals; let alone give you any worthy advice.

This isn't advice on how the CPA works.

It's not asking advice about their client specifically.

For sure do not ask for advice on "how do you like your clients taken care of?"

Don't say, "I was wondering." The CPA has no time for you to ponder.

So what advice are you asking? The kind that makes the CPA know you know *your* stuff, and you are wise enough to know you don't know *their* stuff. Be confident in what you are providing to their client but be sure you know how it needs to fit into the client's tax and financial picture, because anything you do affects it.

Tell the CPA specifically what you are doing with their client and inquire of one simple thing...

To the CPA, "*When we _____ for your client, how do you recommend [client name] pay for it; personally, or through their business?*

That's it. Bold, but simple.

Literally use the word "it." Don't re-describe what you just described. Make what you are selling now an "it."

Example: "When we issue the 20-year term life insurance policy on *your* client, and how do you recommend James pay for **it**? Personally or through their business?"

Don't say "if" we issue it (in that example). Say "when."

Specifically, state "your client," and not their name there. Use the client's name after *recommend.*

You acknowledge your understanding it is *their* client.

When you state the client's name after *recommend* it reminds the CPA subconsciously, it is the client that is paying for this, NOT THE CPA. <u>I am not kidding around here.</u> The CPA can confuse their role sometimes because we are trained to put ourselves in our client's shoes. CPAs sometimes think their advice needs to be consistent with what they would do themselves. Stating it this way reminds the CPA's mind that this is for **their** client.

The combination of this wording is a true combination you need to follow just the same as the sequence to unlock anything.

FOR CLIENTS WHO DO NOT OWN A BUSINESS:

If the client doesn't own a business, you actually have NO advice to ask. Don't ask how the CPA recommends the client pay for it, if they don't own a business because... obviously they will only be paying for it personally.

The other reason you don't need to ask is... unless the client you are working with is massively wealthy, the CPA is typically NOT working closely enough with the client (that only hires the CPA to only prepare their individual return) to know many details about the client outside of what is reported on their tax return. Therefore, you don't want to put the CPA on the spot to even ask about how to pay for it because the CPA simply won't know. You will expose this truth, so to speak, and put the CPA in a negative light.

CPA's that only prepare the personal tax return for a client typically interacts with this client twice a year. Once during preparation time and secondly during year-end or a major event in the client's tax picture (meaning with you).

When preparing the individual return, the CPA doesn't see or need to see bank statements, receipts or any type of monthly statements of any kind *because* they simply only need to see the tax related, annual amounts. This never leads to the CPA in these circumstances knowing account balances (how much money or investments the client has).

Many, including the client, think by preparing a personal tax return the CPA somehow magically also knows everything about them, especially their finances. *Simply not possible.*

Think on this for a minute with your own personal tax returns. The information you use or provide to your tax preparer, how much would anyone know about you? *Not much.*

Therefore, with the CPA who only prepares the individual return, you are possibly creating the only other event the CPA interacts with the client during the year. Therefore, *act accordingly.* Starting with, there is no advice to ask, as in how to pay for it.

NOW BACK TO THE CLIENT WHO DOES OWN A BUSINESS:

You are *not* seeking traditional advice. You are seeking the CPA's *recommendation.* Don't make me, the CPA, feel like I am at any risk. If you do have a question you need advice on, do NOT make it contingent on the CPA. Meaning, ask for a recommendation. We like that word. Do NOT say, "I will do it any way you want." That offends us. We want our client to actually have the final say. We give recommendations to our clients. *Follow?* Do NOT put us on the spot. Ever!

Let me be clear. You are not going to ask, "how will this fit the client's tax and/or financial picture?" We already know that is a question at hand. You asking such a question makes us think you don't know that basics about tax or financial matters, in general. And if you don't know the basics... GET OUT OF HERE!!! That's ignorant on your part. And if you really don't know, I question your

Googling and reading skills. And if you don't know how to Google or read, then ask your superiors or hire your own CPA and find out. *Like do some homework.* No one is expecting you to prepare the tax return, but figure out how your service or product affects your clients taxes. No matter how obscure your service or product is, there has to be at least a hundred articles, YouTube videos, etc. out there telling you how what you do affects taxes. So elevate your game, so you can hang.

When any professional says to me, "I am not a CPA," I literally think you are so ridiculous to point that out to me, because… duh… we all know that. Does a CPA ever say to you, they are not what you are? No.

When a professional says to me, "I don't know taxes," I think of you as lazy.

When a professional says to me, "I know you are the tax expert," it comes across snotty or dumb, take your pick, because that is an obvious we are the tax expert; even if we aren't, we know that's our role, not yours.

When you are talking to your Doctor about a medical issue of yours, do you remind the Doctor you are not a Doctor, you don't know medicine or they are the medical expert? *No?* So why are you doing that with the CPA. STOP IT! When you come to the table, be assured, *we know* you are not a CPA, our role, and what we are an expert in. You are showing zero respect to state any of this. What you are revealing is you are scared of us and/or not confident in what you are getting ready to tell us. **SO KNOCK IT OFF!**

Be confident in yourself, and if you are, we will know that YOU are an expert in what you do starting with the fact you aren't sharing a bunch of dumb statements.

Look at what I underlined in the example from before.

- You acknowledge it is their client.

- You want to *confirm* how the client should pay for it. Confirming means you know it is either personally or through the business. If the CPA mistakes your question as anything but, quickly correct them. Better yet, ask the question quickly so the CPA hears the question in its entirety.

- You are asking for their recommendation (the only advice).

This question will lead to the CPA offering any of the OTHER advice they wish to provide. Believe me, if the

CPA has advice to offer, you will be getting it. Your inquiry signifies to the CPA it is their turn to share any advice they have. *See how you asking for advice without asking for advice?* And please whatever you do, don't actually use the word... *advice.*

Also, this question allows you to know if the CPA is going to put the brakes on it because they will perceive the inquiry as... *this is getting ready to be paid for.* Again, this allows the CPA to directly voice their concerns, and by you knowing their concerns, you will be able to address them, before the actual close.

Next, by receiving the answer, the CPA is telling you they are okay with you (as in you) selling whatever it is, to their client.

Lastly, this avoids the CPA coming across a payment later, for something they weren't expecting and calling the client to figure out what they client was thinking, buying something before talking with them (the CPA).

So much is revealed in that one question; which is the one piece of *advice* you do want to ask for.

"When we _____ for your client, how do you recommend [client name] pay for it; personally, or through their business?

DON'T SAY YOU CAN ADD VALUE

Let's get one thing straight. You cannot and will not add value to a CPA's client. Not possible. (Sarcasm) The only thing of value, is the client. By adding value, you are saying you are going to *add a cost to the client* because you see value completely opposite of the CPA.

Value is code for tricking my client into spending money.

Value is you getting a commission or fee, doing just enough to make yourself feel all warm and fuzzy about it; while my client has had something actually taken away.

Value means you plan to challenge the relationship the CPA has with their client because you think you can be as valuable; or worse, more valuable to the client than the CPA.

This isn't a lack of confidence statement about CPAs. *Quite the opposite.* We know you can't be as valuable as us (the CPA), and we know for dang sure you could never be more valuable than a CPA, because (we believe) there is no other profession that is more valued across the board than CPAs. It is not an opinion; it is a fact. (Sarcasm)

So, your challenge of us would be like a snotty nosed seven-year-old kid challenging a professional athlete to a race. You know that athlete is going to win, but the athlete has to show their client they actually will win. The point is, the exercise would be a total waste of everyone's time. So don't be a seven-year-old and try to challenge the CPA to a race; as in proving you are providing value.

Let me be more plain. <u>Just add value</u>. Don't say you are going to add value. Just add it. Stop saying you are.

Also, when you use the word *"value,"* you are telling the CPA you don't know what the hell you are doing because you can't be more specific than saying *"value."* **So, stop it!**

Stop thinking you bring any *value*. Because you don't.

You are a cost! Recognize it. Own it.

Sarcasm not to be ignored.

On the flipside, a CPA never will call you and say, I think I can add value to your client and would like to show you how. *No way!*

If the CPA wouldn't say what you are saying, then let that be your first clue of what not to say to them.

If you are clueless to what the CPA wouldn't say, then insert the word *Doctor*. If it isn't something you would say to your Doctor, or your Doctor wouldn't say to you, then don't freaking say it!

And if you are still perplexed, think of what you would *and would not* say to Spock. Better yet, what would Spock not say to you.

DO TELL THE CPA WHAT YOU ARE DOING

A CPA would rather you just get to the point and specifically tell them what you plan to do with their client.

I am writing the Will for *your* client.

I am issuing a 20-year term policy for *your* client.

I am installing a new copy, fax and scanning machine for *your* client.

I am investing *your* client in a 20-year fixed indexed annuity.

I am adding an earthquake insurance rider to *your* client's coverage.

I am refinancing *your* client's loan to a 15-year fixed mortgage.

I am putting *your* client in a brand-new car.

See how easy that is. Just tell the CPA. Just lay it out there.

And get to the point why don't you! Don't beat around the bush and give the 15-page proposal, illustration, prospectus, brochure or letter or anything else you think you need to <u>prove</u> to us that what you are doing is right or bringing value. Just spit it out. *Anything else is a cover up!*

Take ownership of it. By saying "I am." The CPA understands, this is all on you *my friend*. This brings the CPA relief that you are doing it, not them. While at the same time making it clear you are doing it to *their* client.

*Also, it is a **bold statement**. Isn't it?* When you state plainly what you are doing to their client, you are providing the CPA with a sense of your confidence.

I can't stress enough, that it is so important to reassure the CPA you understand you see the client as "their client" because then the CPA knows *you know*, it is their client. And don't forget, even if it is a client you referred to the CPA, it is their client; *in their head*. Get over it and go with it. It puts you in a winning position. *You want to close or not? Yes?! Of course, you do!* This is about sharing the language of the CPA, not a contest of ego.

You know darn well they are your client as well. *Be confident with the truth in your own head.*

DON'T ASK FOR A MEETING

A CPA typically makes money by the hour. Meeting with you either costs the CPA lost revenue or the client a bill. Think of your client getting a bill for the time you met with their CPA. Especially if they didn't know you were meeting with their CPA.

When you say, "I would like to schedule a meeting with you [CPA]," you might as well have challenged us to a duel at high noon on main street. You have immediately lead us to believe you are going behind our client's back and you plan to "sell" us, because you haven't sold the client, yet. *You want the client to ask for this meeting!* AND YOU NEED TO INSIST THE CLIENT ATTEND. PERIOD THE END. *NO EXCEPTIONS! NONE!*

Our thought process when you ask for a meeting directly (not the client) is that you are going to come in and waste our time with small talk, trying to make friends with us, while you roll out your slick brochure and present yourself as some kind of pro at what you do, to prove us wrong in what we already know, and that you are just selling something my client doesn't need, want or for sure wouldn't need as much as your selling.

Even if you already have a working relationship with the CPA, you should still follow this protocol because the CPA will always, without a doubt, be loyal to the client first, and not you. The client asking for the meeting changes the entire tone of the request and the actual meeting. (And don't ask to meet with the CPA before the meeting; even if just a few minutes before.)

You asking for the meeting puts us in a <u>spot</u>, as though we have been challenged. **So, don't it!**

The <u>spot</u> is, *who is going to pay us for the time of the meeting?*

Again, we do not feel challenged due to a lack of confidence. Again, quite the opposite. We feel challenged because you are a sales-person, and you probably have already charmed our client like the snake you are (sarcasm), and now if I don't like what you are pitching, I now have to explain to my client *separately* why they shouldn't just fall in love with you, and your idea. Having the client there keeps everyone in their proper roles. Worse, if I like your idea, and I greenlight it, without the client present, if it goes wrong, the client comes right back to me and say, "you told me this was okay," and amazingly they do not usually blame you, the sales-person. Another reason we are so cautious with these matters.

So, asking for a meeting without the client is lost revenue to the CPA and a losing proposition for you.

DO OFFER TO MEET. VERY CAREFULLY.

A CPA may want the opportunity to meet, so you can offer that you are *available* to meet at the CPAs *convenience*, at the CPAs *office* and *pay* for their time if they wish. And always include the client. Always.

Just like any professional, CPAs have relationships with their own clients that differ from client to client. You may have just stumbled upon one of their top clients that they know will pay for their time, or more likely with a top client, that the CPA would want to be fully aware of how all things affect their client as it relates to, typically, their tax picture.

Also, if you simply *offer* to meet, you are now allowing the CPA to decide how to proceed vs. telling the CPA you want to meet with them. By giving the CPA the control in deciding this, you will also get a huge whiff of how the CPA operates with their clients; more specifically, the client you are trying to work with.

If I have control of anything, I am going to be more relaxed, and thus, more open minded. And if the *offer* is to meet at *my convenience*, it shows manners and respect. If the CPA can seal your deal with a nod, you better believe you will meet whenever that CPA is available.

When you actually make the offer that you are available to meet with the CPA, you still want your client to reach out to their CPA to share this. NOT YOU! Be sure to ask your client to include you in the correspondence; best choice being by email. This signals to the CPA, the client is *for* the meeting and by including you, allows the CPA to more easily respond to all parties with any initial questions or concerns. That in itself would be huge to you, to better know how to prepare for the meeting; if it actually occurs.

Side note: If the clients ever asks you to contact the CPA, do it by email, and you MUST include the client. However, if you have never interacted with the CPA, insist the client emails the CPA first. Insist because there will be no deal otherwise. *Insist. Insist. Insist.*

DON'T SAY YOU NEED A CPA RELATIONSHIP

If you are asking for a CPA relationship, you are telling the CPA you have struck out everywhere else, or lying!

I don't know why I have heard this so many times… that someone wants to build or needs a CPA relationship.

Why would you say that out loud? It sounds so desperate!

Would you say to someone, *I need a relationship with a woman/man?* No! You would sound like you had either been washed up or dumped so many times, that you have to just announce, "I need a CPA relationship." *Come on!*

You don't hear someone say, *you know, I need a Dentist relationship. I need a lawn care service relationship.*

More likely, we are going to think you are straight up lying! If you are successful in any way, that means you have been around, and if you have been around, you will have been working with or around CPAs, and you have had plenty of opportunities to work with CPAs, and build a CPA relationship.

Furthermore, who wants to start a relationship with anyone that says, *I need a relationship with you*? Well, that's great, but you would naturally think, what's in it for me. *Follow?* You are already weighing on me. You already want something from me.

I find that most think they are being respectful when they say this. *Well, you are not!* You are being too direct. Too vulnerable. Too needy.

Just let the relationship build naturally. Just like any other. With time, proper nurturing, follow-up, communication and consistency, you will have a relationship with anyone, including the CPA.

Relax! Don't be so obvious!

DO ASK IF THE CPA

IS TAKING ON NEW CLIENTS

If you ask if the CPA is taking on new clients, you are showing respect and making an offering, all in one.

Know this, and believe it. CPAs do NOT need new clients. We value clients. We value new clients. But we do not need more work!

Why? That doesn't even make sense.

If you just thought that, *you a killing me smalls.* You should start this book over. (Sarcasm.)

I will tell you why! Most CPAs don't know how to say no and they find themselves with too many clients.

However, when you ask if they are taking on new clients, you rarely will get a no, but you have got to ask first!

CPAs can only take on as many clients as they can work during a busy season (January 1st to April 15th). There are only so many hours in a day. Only so many staff we can hire to do the work; and those staff can only work so many hours in a day. *Follow?*

More clients does mean more revenue, but the immediate thing a CPA thinks of when you refer a client, good or bad, big or small, rich or poor, the CPA thinks of how much time you are adding to their busy season... how many more hours they are going to have to work... and how many more things they will have to juggle to make the deadlines.

CPAs that are not taking on new clients are the most successful CPAs you will come across. <u>You want to work with that CPA.</u> It makes it easier for you because they will not necessarily want or need referrals from you.

Stop thinking you have some golden nugget to give a CPA because you simply do not.

If you're dealing with big CPA firms that are constantly bringing in young accountants, fresh out of school, then yes, you will find those CPA firms ready to gobble up any and all of your clients that you wish to refer. However, be forewarned, if you are looking to get referrals, you need to do business with CPAs that are ready to do business with you. And thus, with a big CPA firm, you need to make this relationship with a Partner. And let's get real for a minute. Stop thinking you're big time right now if you are creating a relationship with a Partner at a huge CPA firm because a CPA that works with a monster client typically is never going to be the sole decision-maker for that client, let alone for the CPA firm. If you are simply a solo sales-person thinking that you're building a relationship with a CPA who's at a national or regional CPA firm and that you're going to be able to get some big clients out of that, you are kidding yourself and you are wasting your time. There are no elephants to kill with a big CPA firm. Big CPA firms are going to refer to big banks, big law firms, big insurance agencies and huge investment houses. Now, if you represent one of these big companies, this cracking of the code still applies, but you will have train your team to follow your lead and you will need to build a working relationship with the group of CPAs at the big CPA firm. So, get real with what you want and need. The smaller CPA firm and solo CPA is where it's at for most.

NOTE: If the CPA firm has one location, typically, you can find that one CPA in that one CPA firm to work *with*. When there are multiple locations, you better have a team representing your service or product.

DON'T SAY,

I NEED TO REFER CLIENTS TO A CPA

We are busy enough, and stating you are going to refer us clients brings uncertainty, not excitement (unless we have already done a few deals with you).

Most every CPA you come across, probably has too much to do! You thinking you are making an "in" for yourself by making an unspecified promise that you are going to bring more work to the CPAs office is the equivalent of saying, "I have a whole heap of garbage I would like to dump on your desk, and most likely you will find one fresh dollar bill, if you work hard enough to find it."

No thanks!

Referring clients to a CPA is wonderful, thoughtful and appreciated, but unlike most professions, that brings more work, *year after year after year*. Which again, is a great thing, but again, there are only so many hours in the day, and so many ways to service a client effectively. Added to that, there are multiple deadlines a CPA may need to address with a client. So, while one client brings years and years of revenues, it also brings years and years of hours to work, and deadline after deadline to survive. *This makes us very picky!*

With most professions, a client is sometimes only serviced or sold something once, or only periodically; and most likely not with any deadlines (surely not deadlines set by one of the scariest organizations in the world, the IRS).

Many CPAs that have been in practice for any period of time start to gear their services to a certain type of client, with specific services. You stating you have clients to refer, now creates more work for the CPA in just having to sift through the clients you wish to refer, to ensure they are only taking on clients that are a fit.

The general public thinks every CPA does everything related to taxes, accounting, bookkeeping, payroll, sales tax, audits, not to mention anything with money, stocks, retirement, budgeting, etc. etc. *We simply don't do everything.*

So, don't say, "I have clients to refer you" because you just created stress and frustration, and one client hasn't even been referred. Guess how we deal with this stress you brought? We just get rid of YOU! Besides, no offense, we don't believe you because we hear this empty promise all the time.

DO SAY,

I HAVE <u>ONE</u> CLIENT I WANT TO REFER

Hearing you have ONE client to refer sends the message you thoughtfully considered the CPA, as well your client, and the CPA just has ONE decision to make. Easy! Relieving! Welcomed! Appreciated!

You know what sounds lovely? "Hey, I have one client I would like to refer to you. Are you taking on new clients?"

Why am I totally at ease when I write that? First, you are clearly a very thoughtful professional because before you got your client's hopes up that you found them a new CPA, and committed me (before I even have a chance to decide if I have the room for the client) … *you asked.* You have simply asked. *Thank you!*

Second, one client. Easy enough. *I bet I could find room for one more!*

Third, if I have to turn you down, we both will learn something from it, and that will be massively helpful to you (and me) as we move forward.

I will learn what kind of client you are working with, and you will learn what kind of client I want to work with.

Now we are cooking with peanut oil, because you won't try to send clients that are not a fit, and more importantly, you will be referring sweet nectar to the CPA; as long as you continue to not forget to ask *before* you refer.

Remember, there is a reset button with every NEW client that you want to refer to the CPA. Don't assume, now that you know what kind of client the CPA wants to work with you are doing the CPA any favors by now just referring a blanket of clients that you "think" are fit. Most of the time, you are wrong on what is a fit. Meaning, you may not know your client's true needs when it comes to accounting and tax services. Sending a referral to a CPA *without asking* the CPA again, and again, and again, will eventually, and most likely near immediately backfire on you; even if you have been working with that particular CPA for years.

Keep in mind a CPA may work with Doctors, but that doesn't mean they do all tax and accounting services for Doctors. Get it? *Ask, and you shall find!*

DON'T OFFER

TO ADD TO A CPA's BOTTOM LINE

Just don't do it! Ever! Ever! Ever!

You might as well say, "I am going to steal more than I need from your client, so I can share some with you (CPA)."

We make good money! Great money! We don't need yours!

Also, CPAs have to make MASSIVE disclosures to their clients if you offer to share in your revenue; to add to the CPA's bottom line. In fact, we have to disclose to the client BEFORE anything happens that we may share in the revenue of the sale. So, before you breathe a word of the product or service, the commission or fee has to be disclosed to the client. *I ask you, is that really what you want?*

Rest assured, if we know we can share in the revenue, and we see you are gaining a lot of revenue from our clients, if (and I mean if) we want you to add to our bottom line, *we will ask.*

And be super confident in the fact, we will NEVER tell you we can add to your bottom line.

Don't tell the CPA anything they would never tell you.

DO OFFER A <u>DISCLOSED</u> ALLIANCE

What is an alliance?

Exactly! If you offer a <u>DISCLOSED</u> alliance, you and the CPA can open a dialogue about it and you are clearly letting the CPA know, *you know*, it needs to be disclosed.

I have to say though, why in the world would you want to pay me any part of your revenue? *Is it hush money?* See what I mean?

The American Institute of CPAs (AICPA), as well as the State CPA Boards, require massively clear disclosures to clients of the CPA; if they are going to share in any revenue, *whether directly or indirectly*.

DON'T OFFER TO SHARE COMPENSATION

We don't need your money!

Do not insult us!

You're a liar and a cheat (sarcasm), if you're trying to share your compensation!

This means you're making too much money, and our clients are paying more than their fair share; if you're willing to share it with us!

You're trying to make us *make a decision* based on <u>our</u> bottom line, and not on the clients, which is considered evilness to the CPA!

Do you see what a strong reaction that it even gives me, just writing it on this page for you? *Imagine how a CPA feels when you say that to them.*

If the CPA acts like they're interested, they are secretly plotting ways to destroy you as soon as you leave their office; and call every client to warn them about you.

CPAs are passive, nice people with manners, which means we will give you no indication of our displeasure in your offer to help *you* steal from our client.

What we do want is for our client to pay for what they're getting; *and we do want you to make money.* That is NOT a sarcastic statement.

Who do you think understands how money is made more than anybody else? *Great guess.* Yes, the CPA! So, when you walk-in we are already sizing you up with:

- How much do you make?

- How much are you going to charge?

- How are you going to take advantage of our client?

- How are we going to be held responsible to our client if you mess up?

Don't put salt on the wound and offer to share your compensation. What you need to understand is AICPA wants everybody to win, but not at the cost of the client.

The CPA will also think you must be an idiot if you're willing to give up money that you otherwise earned. *So, make the money you're supposed to make!*

DO OFFER TO DISCLOSE

HOW MUCH IT IS GOING TO COST THE CLIENT

What does a client want to know? *What do you want to know when you hire somebody to do anything?* **How much it's going to cost. That is exactly what the CPA wants to know, whether it's for them or their client.** *How much is it going to cost?*

Let's make sure we are on the same page here. Your commission is NOT what you need to disclose as that is NOT actually the cost to the client. What you personally make, is NOT what it is going to cost the client. *Make sense?* Even if you are solo act, say an attorney, and you bill by the hour, and the client is only going to pay you for the time you spend... that is NOT what *you* are going to make. That is what your business is going to make. You have expenses, right? Focus on what it's going to cost the client.

So that is easy, right? Be ready to share with CPA how much it's going to cost their client.

Don't ever say the cost *depend*s. Everything depends! All that means is that you're going to wait to determine how much to *take* the client for a ride, once the CPA gives you the green light.

If it does depend, then break it down to something simple.

An attorney should <u>not</u> say my fee depends on how much time the project takes. **Duh!** Say, our average hourly rate is $250 per hour, and typically this type of project takes approximately 10 hours.   Please do not add some additional disclosure that *it could be more time*. We get what *approximately* means. We are in your same shoes.

A banker should not say we don't charge any fees, or our closing fees depend on the size of the loan. **Duh!** Say our typical fee is 1% of the loan. Please do not say 100 basis points when you mean 1%. Basis points means you are fooling the client with your special jargon the client most likely won't understand. You aren't in a committee meeting with your underwriter. *Speak English!* (Sarcasm that is still true.)

An investment adviser should follow suit with what I just stated for bankers. I charge 1% of assets on a quarterly basis. **Just say it!** And you better never, ever say *basis points*. It's worse coming out of your mouth. Phew! Code word for scam fees! CPAs hate that you charge a percentage. It is seen by the CPA profession as a totally ridiculous way for you to get paid. *Sorry!* (Sarcasm) It would be the same as me saying my tax preparation fee 100 basis points or 1% of my clients AGI (adjusted gross income). And then say, this puts me in line with properly helping the client in that, the lower we make their AGI, the less we make, but the higher we make their AGI, the more we make. It is total hog-wash, crap! But hats off to the investment industry for coming up with this fee structure because many investment advisers make money year after year with no actual incentive to do anything as the fee is based just on what's sitting there. THIS BOOK IS TELLING YOU WHAT CPA's THINK! Doesn't make it true. What's relevant for you, is the CPAs think this. Learn from it. Don't defend it. Just put it out there, when asked. And be done with it.

Insurance professionals. *Well, you are already up a creek with no paddle, with a screen door for the bottom of your boat.* Let's start with this... DO NOT talk about your commission. Don't act like you are enlightening us with what your commission is, and then think it makes you an honest person. We know what you make, and guess what, YOU ARE AN HONEST PERSON. Disclosing what you make doesn't change the fact you are a good, decent human being. Point is, you get no points for sharing here. However, you will get asked, so be ready to disclose it *as a percentage only* and add THAT THE COST OF THE PRODUCT IS THE SAME REGARDLESS OF THE COMMISSION. This is what I recommend, as I am a fellow insurance professional: BEFORE you meet with the CPA, provide anything to the CPA, talk to the CPA, or even look the CPAs direction, have the client complete the underwriting to obtain the rating to then know, *as in know,* what the cost of the product is. If you don't know the rating/premium, and you say, "it depends," you are nothing more than a snake sales-person. HOWEVER, you have the rating, and you know the cost, now you are now *not* selling insurance, you are selling a product, <u>with a clear cost,</u> with a black and white policy. *Make sense?* Now, if you are thinking, but I have to talk with the CPA to know if they will allow the client to buy life, disability income, long-term care insurance, you are, well, a sales-person, and not a professional. Here is my proof of that. An insurance "sales-person," *yes you*, doesn't want to put any work in, unless they know they can close, which makes you a dirty rotten… insurance sales-person. A professional (which is what you actually are) will take the time to have the client go through underwriting before anything is presented to the CPA, which shows the CPA you are a true professional. And from one insurance professional to another, 30% of applicants don't even get approved, right? So, don't step in front of the CPA until you know if the client is approved and what the rating is, i.e. the cost. The rest takes care of itself. Don't get ahead of yourself, even if you think you are saving everyone time. Get the client through underwriting! Furthermore, if your client insists their CPA approve of them getting life insurance, or the amount, you need to do a better job of explaining to your client, there is NOTHING to share (yet) with the CPA, because you don't even know if the client is approved. The CPA is not going to somehow convince your client to proceed through underwriting to find out the cost; that is your job. In short, once you know the cost, then enters the CPA. Period. THE END. Lastly, when presenting the price, use the monthly premium only and break it down into bite-size amounts. Don't confuse everyone with the monthly, quarterly or annual premium. We know how to do math and it doesn't change the CPAs mind to know they save a few bucks paying annually. And when I mean bite-size I mean… it is $14.56 per month for every $100,000 of 10 year term life insurance. This allows the CPA and the client to also use their math skills to calculate out how much $500,000 costs, $1,000,000 costs, etc. KISS! Keep is Simple Stupid. If you don't know what that means… pssst, you missed a chapter.

Okay, where were we?

The fastest way for you to get that coveted green light from the CPA is for you to share with them what it's going to cost their client. The only way you disclose your commission is if that is the actual, total cost to the client and/or the CPA point blank asks.

Don't even act like this is hard or uncomfortable, or you don't know the answer. *It's simple.* If it's not, why are you selling it because you clearly don't know anything then. (Sarcasm? Maybe.)

P.S. Know this. The CPA probably already knows. Just don't act like you don't.

P.S.S. If you actually don't know, then you aren't ready to meet with the CPA, and tell your client it's not time to meet with the CPA.

P.S.S.S. However, don't use this as an excuse to not meet with the CPA, because if you wait too long, you will get burned. U*se common sense here.*

DON'T STOP BY

You clearly have nothing better to do if you're going to just stop in on a CPA.

You're clearly up to something if you're *just stopping by*.

You're not going to catch us with a moment to spare, *and if you do, you just wasted the <u>one</u> moment we have to spare.*

Honestly, it is rude that you think you can just stop by and interrupt our day, without an appointment. **So don't do it!**

Do you like it when someone knocks on your door at your house on a Saturday whether it's 9:30 a.m. or 3 p.m.? When you see someone standing at your door (that you aren't expecting), whether you recognize them or not, what goes through your mind? Don't even tell me for one second that you're going to holler at your family and say, "guess who it is!"

You are in grubby's, teeth not brushed, hair not done, enjoying some peace and quiet on Saturday…

KNOCK, KNOCK!

That's what it's like when you just stop by our office.

Something else: Our office… is more like our home. Meaning the CPA spends a lot of time at their office and it can easily become their second home. *So, treat it as such.*

The best way to show your "bad manners" is to show up unannounced and make the poor soul who had to greet you (the receptionist) go back and ask the CPA, "are you expecting this *salesperson?*"

PAUSE: See what just happened there? You just got labeled my friend!

Know what happens next? The CPA might bark at the person asking (maybe) because if the CPA was expecting you, they would have communicated that somehow to the front person... so you make everyone doubt the office's system for expecting someone. And/or, the CPA has to figure out what excuse to give. Then, the person has to return to you (that may have just been barked at) and give you "the excuse" why the CPA can't see you.

PAUSE: So... what kind of impression do you think you are setting here? *This working in your favor at all?*

Then what happens? The receptionist is going to know you're a clown because you are clearly someone that doesn't know how to conduct business with the CPA. You'll be the laughing stock of the CPA's office as soon as you walk out the door, and worse, all your mail and messages will be further scrutinized. I am not going to lie, I have told my front people... *the next time they...* <u>fill in the blank</u>. Why? Because, again, you clearly have no clue on how to communicate with a CPA, and there are so many of you stopping by, that it becomes comical. That's how you get put in the "little car" with all the other *clowns!*

Guess how you be different? Don't just stop by!

DO *SNAIL MAIL* US

WHAT YOU WOULD DROP BY

CPAs get nothing but IRS letters, tax documents, requests from banks, client correspondence and bills in the mail, as in snail mail that comes in paper form in envelopes that have to be opened from a mailbox.

What you would drop by most likely is shiny and eye catching, because that's why you wanted to personally drop it by.

Think how magnificent the contents of your envelope will be when it shows up in the CPAs mailbox; <u>especially if hand-addressed to the CPA</u>

You probably hate traditional mail. But remember CPAs are not in this century. We still enjoy the feel of paper between our fingers vs. view documents on a computer screen.

We value the mail. We trust the mail. The mail is less suspect. The mail has been around since before the CPA designation was created. We trust the mail person that delivered it. We trust the mail person that picks up our mail. We trust the postage. We trust the return address. We trust the address an envelope is addressed to. We mail documents to the IRS and other governmental agencies everyday. We mail our invoices to clients. We mail tax returns and reports to clients. Do you see where I'm going with this? *Your mail falls in the category of something a CPA already trusts.*

Yes, CPAs do use email and do like PDFs as well as paperless documents. As an industry, we are moving very much to using all virtual communication and documentation, but that does not change the fact that the CPA, a traditional, successful CPA enjoys mail that is not the typical mail. When I get something from anybody that is not typical mail, my staff brings it to me immediately, with a smile and excitement that it's shiny! Especially from the "pen company!"

If you are dealing with the CPA firm that is paperless (mine), they still love mail! Even more so!

NOTE: What experience level do you think the CPA has, that is the referring CPA? The new CPA that loves everything done in a "app?" Or the CPA that is running things, i.e. been around the block, doing this for awhile?

See where I am going with this? The experienced CPA is who you are trying to CRACK THE CPA CODE with, and they traditionally like mail, and paper.

DON'T BRING US FOOD & GIFTS IN APRIL

We don't want to see anybody for the entire month of April.

The days in April leading up to the deadline are our craziest. The days after the deadline in April is our time to recover from the tax-marathon, and we need the rest of April for that.

Stay completely clear of the CPA during April. PERIOD.

Pretty much any CPA is busy in April.

CPAs involved in audits are busy to get those complete, so the tax returns can be completed.

CPAs in the large companies, referred to as being in industry, are busy getting documents to the external CPAs to complete audits and tax returns.

And do I even need to mention that CPAs in a tax practice are busy in April?

The worst thing you can do is hiccup in front of a CPA in the month of April.

If you need anything from a CPA, you better get it before April 1st, and after April 30th, if you want to gain or maintain a positive relationship with a CPA. *Respect it!* Don't think you're special. Don't think you're the exception. Even if the CPA says, "that's okay," that is secret code for I will go ahead and get this done for you and then you are on *my list*.

Think if you in the middle of a heavy workout of any kind. A physical workout. While you're in the workout or recovering, is that when you want to talk about something that can wait? *Don't test us!*

Now, did you pick up that I said April? I did NOT say April 15th. After April 15th, we just finished our marathon, our workout that was 100 days long. *No!* We are not wanting to meet with you the last 2 weeks of April. *No!* We do not want to schedule anything before April 15th, even for something after April 15th *that is in April.* A runner needs time to catch their breath, cool down, shower, rest, relax and recover. The CPA is the same. Are you going to get the best reaction or interaction with the CPA during that time-period? Clearly not! *No matter what you think.*

DO BRING US FOOD & GIFTS IN FEBRUARY

Many people and businesses want to bring gifts to CPAs, and it's very sweet and thoughtful.

However, it goes completely unnoticed when you deliver it in April, especially on April 15th, because we are BUSY!

Many CPAs already have lined up meals and gifts for their staff, so you are actually and directly competing with the CPA. *Dumb, dumb, dumb!*

In February, it will be noticed and appreciated! <u>In February, you will be the ONLY one bringing gifts!</u>

CPAs definitely appreciate being appreciated with meals and gifts, especially if you include enough for the entire staff. It is very gracious and kind. The CPAs, especially the smaller CPA firms, actually don't get this treatment often. So these CPA firms will really appreciate your gestures.

In February CPAs are just ramping up and are just starting to work overtime, and meals are greatly appreciated because most firms have yet to start planning to provide such things. Therefore, you will be the only one providing smiles and cheer. No one. And I mean no one has ever brought me or my firm anything in the month of February. Can you imagine how much you would stand out if you did that for me after all these years in practice? (Over 27 years in practice, and NO ONE has acted in February.)

P.S. Do yourself a favor and do not leave pens! UNLESS THEY LIGHT UP!

Donuts. Sandwiches. Pizza. Cupcakes. **Things eaten on the go!** *Eaten at the desk!* <u>**Finger foods!**</u> *Follow?*

Rulers. Mouse pads. Flashlights. Highlighters. Small notepads. USB or flash pen. Action figures. Golf balls and tees. Yes! Yes! Yes! Fun! Fun!

DON'T BRING US

GIFTS 6 MONTHS OUT OF THE YEAR

There are 6 months with key deadlines!

FYI: Major deadlines are always on the 15th, or the equivalent.

We have zero time to waste leading up to the deadline.

We are seriously recovering the 15 days after!

We don't like people in general. (Sarcastic)

We really don't like people in these months!

Don't bring gifts in March.

(Business tax deadline.)

Don't bring gifts in April. PERIOD.

(You should know better!)

Don't bring gifts in May.

(We need an extra month to recover!)

Don't bring gifts in September.

(Business extension deadline.)

Don't bring gifts in October.

(Individual extension deadline.)

Don't bring gifts in December.

(Year-end tax planning.)

Like, with all due respect, *leave us be*, during these months!

We love gifts, but your gift can't be special enough, and unless it is a gift that will allow the CPA, EA or accountant to walk away with enough money to retire on the spot, the moment you give this gift, your gift will not be as appreciated or as recognized. *You want your gifts to be recognized, right?*

NOTE: You are in the middle of giving birth or passing a kidney stone, at what point in time, while trying to pass this foreign object out of your body, would you want to receive a gift. And once you passed it, how soon after would you care about receiving a gift?

Want your gift remembered? Pick the right time!

DO BRING US

GIFTS 6 MONTHS OUT OF THE YEAR

These months do not have key deadlines!

We are happier these months, with no major deadlines.

We have time to waste. (Sarcastic)

We are at the office, but in a relaxed state!

We actually like people. *I was just kidding from before.*

Remember these months!

Do bring gifts in January.

(Everyone else gave to us in December.)

Do bring gifts in February.

(The flood has not started.)

Do bring gifts in June.

(A wonderful month. We've seen the sun by then.)

Do bring gifts in July.

(Popular vacation month, but we are happy!)

Do bring gifts in August.

(Maybe only through the 3rd week.)

Do bring gifts in November.

(It is the golden month for us.)

If you are going to take the time to bring a gift, you definitely want it to be well received, recognized and appreciated. *That is the whole point, right?* So, knowing the key months to bring us a gift will lead to you being known as not only generous, but someone "who knows the CPA & accounting industry." We like that. We like for you to know when it is a good time to bring us gifts, as in we like for you to know our kind.

The months to bring us gifts… think of as business hours. If you are bringing a gift to anyone, and I mean anyone, a gift in the morning or afternoon is going to be received way better than you delivering it at midnight or 5 am, right?

DON'T TAKE YOUR COMMUNICATION WITH A CPA LIGHTLY, AND DO EXPECT A CPA WILL REMEMBER HOW YOU COMMUNICATED WITH THEM, AS WELL AS WHEN

What's key for you to remember is that when you're communicating with the CPA, they are taking in everything. They are paying attention to the WWWWWH of what you are communicating because CPAs are trained to exercise professional skepticism. *Remember professional skepticism?*

The CPA always has their antennas up to figure out what somebody's actually trying to do because the CPA is expected to know a little bit (not a lot) about everything.

<u>This puts the CPA in a position of *defense* pretty much all the time.</u>

The CPA sees themselves as the gatekeeper to their clients… on just about everything in their financial picture; even though most CPAs only deal directly with a client on one of the financial aspects of their client's lives.

The key thing to note here is that CPAs are blamed and sued everyday by clients who *thought* their CPA was either helping them with some aspect of their financial picture, that they never engaged the CPA to do, or that the CPA should have warned them; even if the CPA was not aware of the issue at hand.

That sounds unbelievable doesn't it? It is amazing how much clients expect the CPA to know about their financial dealings. *Why is this?*

When we are doing the client's books, we see their bank statements.

When we are doing their tax returns, we see where they make money, how they make money and how much money they make.

When we are doing their business tax return, we see potentially who their clients are and what banks they bank with and where their loans are.

Most likely a CPA interacts at some time or another with the client's attorney, banker, investment advisor, insurance professional or others that the client asks the CPA to interact with.

If a CPA audits the client, they are interacting with all of the above.

This puts the CPA many times in a position of knowing more about the client than anyone else; which mistakenly leads the client to thinking the CPA knows as much as them. The real problem there is that clients then expect the CPA to know more what *to do* with the financial aspects of their lives because the CPA is seen as an expert in everything related to money.

So, when the CPA is communicating with you, they are naturally and instinctually on the defense, ready to be blamed, expected to already know everything you plan to interact with the client on.

Your communication needs to be done thoughtfully, carefully and *with due care.*

Your communication is best shared in a manner that the CPA can refer back to and document their file with. And this does NOT include your sales presentation. I mean the final product. The CPA usually has a heightened sense of tracking paperwork and communication. Make it easy for them to incorporate it into their file.

A few things to consider:

When you send something in the mail, this is going to require the CPA and their staff to open it, figure out who should deal with it and where to file it. Therefore, make it clear who in the CPA's office you expect to handle it, and who the mutual client is.

If you are mailing a final product, plan, or document, first email the CPA to give them a heads up it is coming.

When you send something bound, the staff has to unbound it. *Guess what?* Don't send something bound.

When you drop off a brochure, that shiny trifold, it cannot be scanned properly because it won't be in order.

A brochure is not informational to a CPA because it's simply is a sales piece. A sales piece pieces make great promises but leaves great detail out. This is problematic.

A brochure that highlights all the benefits and leaves out details immediately puts the CPA in a position to be held responsible; not to mention allows the CPA to know what the negatives are and pre-warn the client. *Is that what you want?* You are NOT selling what you are selling to the CPA, so don't approach the CPA the way you would approach your client.

When you communicate with a CPA without the client present or involved directly, you are increasing the CPA's liability in appearance and in fact. The client will expect the CPA to have heard, considered, examined, and discerned every aspect of what you are telling them from A to Z, as well as all the fine print.

Emailing a CPA and including the client allows the CPA to feel included but not taking on the responsibility outside of their scope of services to the client; even though clients will still hold the CPA responsible for anything you do with *their* client.

A CPA also will closely pay attention to *when* you are communicating, as it will be an indicator of how you do business and how you are communicating with *their* client.

CPAs are in a traditional profession that includes traditional communication, such as a greeting and a close to communication.

CPAs communicate typically during traditional business hours.

The CPA will pay attention to how much time you give them and *their* client to respond to your communication.

Meaning if you're communicating right before your deadline, the CPA sees that you're putting a sense of urgency on them for something they don't do for the client, but more what a CPA will note is, you're pressuring their client with a tight deadline.

Communicating in advance of what needs to be done allows the CPA time to communicate with their client if necessary and keep things relaxed for *their* client.

You need to remember that with one word from the CPA your client will *or will not* do your deal, buy your product, or continue to do business with you.

The CPA may have nothing to do with what you are selling to their client but if they don't like you or think you are a shuckster, the CPA absolutely will say something to their client; and most likely that client will listen to the CPA before they listen to anybody else in their life.

The CPA is in the most powerful position with your client. Your communication can make *or break* your deal.

Again, what's key for you to remember is that <u>when</u> you're communicating with a CPA; they are taking in everything.

Here are a few more items to consider:

Don't go overboard with your *promises*.

Don't be vague.

Respect the position they have with *their* client.

Respect them.

Communicate to your (their) client, and let the CPA listen in.

Interact with the CPA like you would your grandparents, with great respect and thoughtfulness. Without rush or irritation. With wonderful manners and care. With generosity, taking your time. Ensuring they are on the same page with you. *And then with that image in mind, remember, grandparents are always there for you, right?*

The best situation you can be in, is for the CPA you are dealing with to become like a grandparent to you. Once the CPA becomes loyal to you, you will have it for as long as you deserve it, and at some point you will become their favorite... most likely only wanting to help you (not that other guy/gal)… as long as you continue to "help them walk across the street."

RAPID FIRE!

DO's!

Don'ts!

Don't write a snail mail letter if it requires a response.

Don't send an information packet.

Don't drop by a brochure.

Don't take more than 5 minutes to explain a concept.

Don't bring color printed materials.

Don't bring brochures.

Don't send a bound copy of your plan.

Don't leave a voicemail asking the CPA to call you.

Don't ask the assistant to provide anything to you.

Do write an email.

Do send a summary of your services.

Do email a link to your electronic brochure.

Do take a minute to describe each concept.

Do bring black and white printed materials.

Do bring your business card.

Do send a send a bound copy to your client.

Do send an email asking to visit with the CPA.

Do leave a message for the appropriate person to call.

Don't explain a concept for general purposes.

Don't "start at the beginning."

Don't start with the benefits.

Don't start with your background.

Don't tell a CPA your credentials.

Don't tell the accountant or CPA you can share revenue.

Don't ask for a referral.

Don't ever ask for a referral.

Do explain the exact concept that applies.

Do start with the end-result.

Do end with the benefits.

Do share your background, if and when asked.

Do list your credentials in your email signature.

Do see the door hitting your backside if you mention fee sharing.

Do a good job, and you will probably get a referral.

Do a great job, and you will get a referral.

A SINGLE WORD

CAN MAKE OR BREAK YOU

We've all heard the saying, "a picture is worth a thousand words." Know this, one word could mean a thousand things to anyone else, but NOT to the CPA.

What do I mean?

There are keywords in a CPA's vocabulary. There are very sensitive words that when a CPA hears them *a 5 alarm fire siren goes off.* It's a situation where the CPA goes into a one-track mind of your motive, or what you expect of the CPA.

What am I talking about here?

When you say loosely, "we're going to *audit* this." The CPA immediately thinks of a financial *audit* which is the most stressful engagement a CPA can undertake because of all of the procedures, requirements, expectations, and responsibilities the CPA has, when involved with an *audit*.

The CPA is not going to think you are considering the word *audit* in any other way.

It's the same thing when you use the word ***review***. A CPA using the word *review* means that they looked at the information with great care and detail, as well as consideration of all aspects to arrive at a conclusion that the CPA will be held responsible for to third parties, i.e. people the CPA doesn't even know.

Are you still lost? Wake up! Right now!

You need to focus in on the words that you are using with a CPA. Don't be confused on these two words especially: audit and review. <u>Don't forget either!</u>

Ever seen a bull get hopping mad? There is no convincing that bull of anything. You can't reason with it. A bull becomes a one-track mind, which is... charge... run over... and take out whatever is in front of it (you).

Not only will you have made the CPA mad, you will have shown the CPA you have no idea what you are doing because only a CPA can conduct an audit or review; at least the kind we are thinking of.

Words in our profession have specific meanings with very *specific responsibilities*. Specific words describe an engagement, the services the CPA is providing. Specific words potentially expand a CPAs engagement with their client. A CPA does not just do anything a client wants them to do. We are trained to be very specific with our *scope* of services to clients; as it's part of our responsibilities to maintain being a CPA. Don't get us out of the *scope* of services we already defined with our client, which you have successfully done by uttering the words *audit* or *review*.

When you ask the CPA, "will you review this and get back to me?" you are asking the CPA to do more than you think; and you are then creating way more stress than you intended, putting the CPA in a position of defense. Not to mention, you are asking the CPA to do something outside of the *scope* of their services to the client. *Why would you do that?* You wouldn't. At least, you didn't realize you did, but that's what you did by simply saying, "will you review this?"

There are other words that are used and thrown around by those outside of the CPA industry that drive us bananas because it is shucksters and sales-persons pretending to be something that they are not, and/or pretending to do something they don't actually intend to do.

Ready?

And by the way… if you take issue with these words, you are asking for trouble and a fight you are going to lose. *Just accept it.*

When you say you're going to take a *holistic approach* or you are doing a *comprehensive* review, you are sending the

CPA to the moon with not only *professional skepticism* of what you're actually up to but with great stress on your expectations of them, and more serious, the expectations you are placing on the client to have of you. *Why? How?* Because for you to have this "so called" holistic or comprehensive review, you are going to require I provide information to you I may not want to share, ask I make projections (which we are disallowed from doing) and/or agree with your silly, silly projections. And more to the point, you are just doing this to sell the client something else in the end.

PAUSE: If you don't use the word holistic or comprehensive, keep reading and see my special note for you at the end of this chaper.

While you want the CPA to be involved with the process, you don't need to, and you should not, put the CPA in the position to actually make any decisions; other than what? *Do you want your client to pay for it personally or through their business?*

With that being said, the CPA has a great respect for the words used in these examples (holistic, comprehensive, audit, review), and if you *toss them around*, you are telling the CPA you do not have respect for these words which equates to you giving the impression you don't have respect for the CPA.

I'm not saying the CPA thinks you are disrespecting them. I'm saying that when you greatly appreciate and admire someone, you show them great respect. *Right?* And in showing respect, you use the right language. The right words.

So, get in tune with what the CPA <u>is hearing</u>. *With the words you are saying or writing.*

Do you cuss around your grandparents? Okay, maybe you do. Do you cuss around someone else's grandparents? See, you have the ability to change your words, or at least filter them. Remember, the CPA profession is similar to interacting with grandparents.

I'm telling you this right now, anybody that uses the word *holistic*, I don't even want to know them. 99.9% of CPAs don't want to know this person. I don't want to have anything to do with them! There is salesperson! There is a shuckster! It's total baloney. They're a fake *feel good* and emotional salesperson. **They're going to take advantage of my client!!!** *See what I mean?*

HERE IS WHY: It's not possible to be *holistic* enough, in the CPA's mind, and so this person is basically a liar and what they're going to do is hogwash.

Sure. That is an opinion!

Guess what?

I am testing you right here.

You feeling a little frustrated or irritated that I am going on and on about the word holistic? *Good.* Then you are learning something. About CPAs. About your approach.

And guess what else? If you are frustrated about this discussion about the word holistic, you have proven my point that you are in this for yourself. You came up with some ridiculous word you fell in love with, and you are going to ruin a whole relationship with a CPA over it, which means you could care less about the client.

Yes. Sarcasm, but this is what is going through a CPAs mind. *Follow?*

Okay, let's continue, because you aren't getting off this easy. I am giving you the secrets of working with the CPA, and I want you to be worthy of it. I am not kidding around. No sarcasm. Well, maybe a little.

I digress…

Someone saying holistic means that they're going to grossly over charge for their services because they're leaving the *impression* that they're going to do all this work for the client.

Someone who says holistic is using a new word which is a fad. CPAs are driven by tradition, and well proven concepts which includes traditional words.

Now I'm talking about in the financial world.

Doctors that use the word holistic, don't conjure up these images or emotions for CPAs; most likely. *So, hear me.* One word can make or break you on a deal *with* the involvement of a CPA.

I don't need you to think that you should be petrified and nervous to communicate to a CPA, but I am saying that you should use great care in the words you choose so that you are putting yourself in the best position to do business with the CPA.

If you want to approach it like a salesperson, then think of it as any other approach you have with a client. You use certain words to evoke emotion in the sales process. *Do the opposite with a CPA.*

You use tactics with a client to get them to make a decision. *Do not use those tactics with the CPA.*

You follow up with clients and potential clients in a way to build a personal relationship in some regard. *Don't do that with a CPA.*

Not until they start doing that with you.

Let the CPA make the first move!

There will come a time that you will have a well-established relationship with a CPA and you will see they will relax and not be as concerned with the words that you are using because they will then know what you mean by them. But until then, consider using the words with the CPA like you would with an elementary school kid.

Now that sounds funny, doesn't it?

What I mean by that is that when you're communicating with a young person you usually are considering that they're not going to understand your jargon or sales talk.

So when a fourth grader asks you what you do, you would not say, "I take a *holistic and comprehensive approach* with my clients to do an *analysis* and a financial *plan* to serve as an external CFO, so that I can *share revenue* with CPAs because I *guarantee* that when I *review* the clients results and I make a projection, CPAs will want to partner with me."

You would say, "I sell insurance. I'm an attorney. I'm a foot doctor. I sell appliances. I'm a software developer."

I'm not being disrespectful to the CPAs by saying that you have to dumb it down for us, but what I am saying is *dumb it down for us*. That way we will not be suspicious of your intentions.

CPAs are trusting human-beings when born, but until you get through the exterior of the CPA, your words determine if and when you will experience the human side of the CPA.

I put together some examples of words and know these are the most keywords you do NOT want to use.

If you come up with some other word, it needs to be simple, leaving very little to the imagination of what your word means.

SPECIAL NOTE: For those that don't use the word *holistic* or *comprehensive*, while I love you, you aren't off the hook with this chapter. What you want to pay attention to with the CPA you are working with is... is there a word you use that they react to like I did with holistic? *Follow?*

WORDS

You're going to see my list of words that you do NOT want to use.

I would like to reiterate the words you should never use.

AUDIT.

REVIEW.

COMPILATION.

The biggest reason why is that you will never be qualified to do what it is these words actually mean because only a CPA is actually able to do these three things above. Don't use these above words. Ever. Never. Ever! Don't even kid around about these above words by saying, "I know you don't like others to use the word audit, but... I am an idiot and I am going to anyway."

You might as well say to the next over-weight person you meet, "I know you don't like others to use the word *fatso*, but I am an idiot and I am going to anyway."

Follow?

DON'T

use these words.

DO

use these words.

Don't use the word "guarantee."

Don't use the word "audit."

Don't use the word "review."

Don't use the word "projection."

Don't use the word "comprehensive."

Don't use the word "compilation."

Don't use the word "holistic."

Don't use the word "process."

Don't use the word "analysis."

Do use the word "probable."

Do use the word "looked over."

Do use the word "looked over." (Yes, the same word.)

Do use the words "estimated."

Do use the word "complete."

Do use the word "gathered."

Do use the word that doesn't mean you are a phony.

Do use the word "produce."

Do use the word "conclusion."

Don't use the words "financial plan."

Don't use the word "external CFO."

Don't use the words "IRS."

Don't use the words "Line 19."

Don't use the words "IRC code section ____."

Don't use the words "revenue sharing."

Don't use the word "associate" referring to the CPA.

Don't use the words "partner with CPAs."

Do use the words to describe the <u>kind of</u> "plan."

Do use the word "adviser."

Do use the words "government."

Do use a word that doesn't specify a line item.

Do use the words "according to our interpretation."

There is no "do" here. Only if the CPA brings it up.

Do use the word "team."

Do use the words "work with CPAs."

Don't wait more than a week to follow up.

Don't ask to meet this week.

Don't *ask* to meet for lunch.

Don't *ask* to meet for coffee.

Don't *ask* if you can bring in lunch to meet.

Don't *ask* if you can bring in coffee & donuts to meet.

Don't *ask* to meet for drinks.

Don't *ask* to meet for dinner.

Don't *ask* to meet with them first thing in the morning.

Do follow up when you say you will.

Do *offer* to meet next week. *Always next week.*

Do *offer* to meet for lunch <u>or at their office..</u>

Do *offer* to meet for coffee <u>or at their office..</u>

Do *offer* to bring in lunch <u>or just meet at their office.</u>

Do *offer* to bring in coffee & donuts <u>or at their office.</u>

Do *offer* to meet for drinks <u>or at their office.</u>

Do *offer* to meet for dinner <u>or at their office.</u>

Do *offer* to meet <u>at their office.</u>

See any themes there?

When you ask, you force the CPA to make a decision. That is very forward. It is not polite.

When you offer, the CPA isn't forced to make a decision. That is simple. Easy.

It is the subtleness that is the key!

Don't *ask* to meet with the CPA at the end of the day.

Don't say you can put on an event for their clients.

Don't say you offer CPE (continuing professional education).

Don't ask if you can meet with them without *their* client.

Don't show up and expect to meet with the CPA.

Don't ever, ever just show up unannounced.

Don't stop by.

Do *offer* to meet <u>at their office.</u>

There is no "do" to offset this one.

There is no "do" to offset this one. We will see it as a sales pitch. We don't need free CPE. It always sucks!

Do offer to meet with them with *their* client. And then do that.

Do plan on NOT meeting with the CPA; maybe ever.

Do plan to be shunned by their office if you do.

There is no "do" to offset this one, unless you are only dropping something off (not asking to even say "hi.").

Don't "just be in the neighborhood."

What ones do you have?

Don't _____.

Don't _____.

Don't _____.

Don't _____.

There is no "do" on this one. *No one is just in the...*

What ones do you have?

Do _____.

Do _____.

Do _____.

Do _____.

AND DON'T DO THESE

Don't call or email a CPA the 5th-15th of any month.

Don't ask for quarterly financials at the end of the quarter. How is it possible they are done before the quarter ends? Or even within days of the quarter ending. *Think!*

Don't send duplicate bank or investment statements to the CPA. Creates massive liability for the CPA, as the client can prevail later in assuming the CPA examined each statement, and approved of everything done with the account. *Not kidding!*

Don't take no for an answer.

Don't accept the first response.

Don't expect the CPA is making money taking your call.

Don't make small talk with a CPA until you know them.

Don't ask how long they have practiced.

Don't ask for a meeting to be <u>sometime</u> Tuesday afternoon. *Get specific.*

Don't be late. Don't be early.

Don't wear jeans. (On the first visit with the CPA.)

Don't wear tennis shoes.

Don't open up your iPad or laptop during a meeting.

Don't tell jokes.

Don't put your picture on your business card.

Don't ignore the value of the plain business card.

Don't expect the CPA to have looked at your website.

Don't expect them to like you.

Don't try to find things in common.

Don't give a pencil.

Don't give a pen. (Unless it lights up.)

Don't ask for a donation. *We don't have money to throw away.*

Don't tell the CPA who your clients are. *You just told us you know nothing of confidentiality.*

Don't assume a CPA cares about a tax deduction.

Don't tell a CPA something is tax deductible. *How the heck do you know!*

Don't go dutch treat. Unless they insist. Otherwise buy lunch, dinner, or golf. If they have a reason they don't want you to do that, they will tell you.

Don't think a CPA respects frugal. I have 3 Rolex watches and drive a brand-new Jaguar. HELLO!!!

Don't say, *before you get busy*. Phew! Makes me see red to read it.

Don't let your client explain to the CPA what you are doing, if you can help it. Ask the client, if you can share with the CPA (and include the client).

Don't ask the CPA to call the banker.

Don't ask the CPA to send anything client related to you. We cannot send anything directly to a 3rd party with out specific, written consent by the client, specific to each and every need. IRS disallows this. It goes to the client, then the client sends to you. PERIOD!

Don't talk to the CPA without the client; whether in person or on the phone.

Don't email the CPA without cc'ing the client. Don't freaking do it! Not even to say, "thanks for your time." You are inviting the CPA to converse with you, without their client.

Don't tell a CPA you told the client to check with you.

Don't expect we know everything. Set up for disaster. If you expect, CPAs feel they need to. Shows your ignorance too.

Don't tell the CPA they are the expert in tax.

Don't tell the CPA they are the expert in audit.

Don't tell the CPA they are the expert in cost accounting.

Don't tell the CPA they are the expert on budgeting.

Don't tell the CPA they are the expert on real estate.

Don't tell the CPA they are the expert about insurance.

Don't tell the CPA they are the expert about investments.

Don't tell the CPA they are the expert about estate planning.

Don't tell the CPA they are the expert with anything!

We determine what we are an expert in. You don't expect your Dentist to be an expert in determining if your foot is broken, or if you have skin cancer. *Follow?*

Don't ever, ever, ever say... I've <u>never</u> heard of a CPA who didn't know this. *Oh my, those a fightin' words!*

Don't ever, ever, ever say... I talked to my CPA and they said this was okay. <u>*Get out of here. SCRAM!!!*</u>

Don't ever, ever, ever say... this is really simple; it will be easy for you. *Are you freaking kidding me right now?*

SO WHERE DO I FIND THIS ONE CPA?

Where do you find such a CPA? Well, they are right there in front you. Right in your hometown.

Take your pick because I can near guarantee of all the CPAs you can list, maybe one of them has a relationship with someone like you, in the manner you are getting ready to have with them.

This means the playing field is wide open my friend!

But let me keep on truckin' with the theme of numbers.

HUNT DOWN, TRACK AND FIND THE FOLLOWING:

30   List out 30 CPAs in your area.

20   Qualify down to 20, contact and refer to the CPA.

10   Narrow down to the 10 CPAs that respond.

3   Narrow down to the 3 CPAs that will work for you.

1   Narrow down to the CPA that refers 1 client to you.

3   Refer 3 more clients or prospects to that 1 CPA.

10   Have 10 non-client interactions with that 1 CPA.

20   Have 20 *client* interactions with that 1 CPA.

30   Maintain 30 interactions with that 1 CPA annually.

You need to accomplish all those steps, except the last one, within 6 months.

Sounds like some work. Heck yeah! You are searching for the golden goose! *Totally worth it.*

I'm going to walk you through a plan of action. Then, follow the principles, timing, language, coupled with referring 4 clients to that one CPA you find; keeping momentum that you will not falter from.

Now let me preface all of this by saying if you think that you can build a relationship with a CPA in the next six weeks and get referrals inside of eight, you are setting yourself up for disappointment. You need to invest 6 months of your time into that one CPA and then another year to accomplish the full CPA code being cracked.

You need to be in this for the long haul, and by being in it for the long haul, well, that in itself will prove to the CPA you're trying to build relationships. That you will be around. You will be reliable and will be there to take care of their clients, that you share in common with the CPA.

This isn't a game.

<u>This isn't a tactic.</u>

This is called a strategy.

What you're getting ready to embark on is a proven method to create a foundation to elevate you to the next level in your career, which is to say the proverbial… *Rome was not built in a day.*

Ready? Good!

Now open your mind and stop thinking you have this all figured out. Because you don't! You are about done with this book, but your real task is to crack the CPA code with one CPA. Just one CPA. And you will. Then you will successfully be on your way to building a long lasting, mutually beneficial relationship with that one CPA, while all your peers will sit in wonderment of how you are creating the success that you will most definitely experience.

PLAN OF ACTION:

___ List 30 CPAs that you know or a CPA that someone you know, knows. Don't just get a list from Google.

I recommend you find CPAs that are your age or up to 10 years older than you. These need to be CPAs that are owners of the CPA firm. Your best bet is a one owner CPA firm, or solo practitioner.

___ Research those 30 CPAs to narrow it down to 20 CPAs that you pre-qualify as fitting your needs, or more importantly, the needs of your clients. Look at their experience level and see who else they are connected with through social media connections, especially LinkedIn.

__ Refer one of your clients (or prospects) to those 20 CPAs using the principles I laid out for you. Until you find the one CPA, your client will not meet, know the CPA or even be aware of this process, so don't get caught up with this *other than* you want to refer your *sweet spot* client, as you are trying to find that *sweet spot* CPA.

__ Narrow down to the 10 CPAs that respond within 5 days of your referral. Regardless of the response, positive or negative; if you got a response, they make the cut to your list of 10 CPAs.

__ Connect with the CPA about your referral, providing details of your client (not the clients name at this time) to see what kind of fit this is for you and the CPA. You are further qualifying the CPA. Refer back to my Do's and Don'ts as you are NOT interviewing the CPA. You are simply letting them know the details of your client to see if they are able to take on this one client. You should already know the CPA's background, what their area of expertise is and have a flavor for their personality.

___ Refer your client (or prospect) to 3 the CPAs from the list of 10 that you feel comfortable with, and that you believe will work well *with you.*

___ See which CPA lands your client (or prospect), and everything the CPA did to land your client (or prospect). This will allow you to learn so much about the CPA. Again, go back to my principles and see what applies to this particular CPA. Now you are dealing with a real-live CPA, and this is where you will see who you are dealing with.

__ Follow my principles to be a part of all the steps the CPA takes to land your client. Be at every meeting and included in all communications. Don't sell the CPA to your client. See which CPA sells themselves.

__ With the CPA that lands your client, continue to work "with" that CPA. Continue the process of now being involved, included and/or aware of the what the CPA is now doing with your client. You want to stay present to constantly remind the CPA (without saying it) that you referred them a client.

__ With the CPA that landed your client, have 10 non-client interactions that have nothing to do with referring a client, or getting a client referred. These 10 interactions cannot include sales pieces or discussions on what you do or how you work. You are NOT telling the CPA anything about your job, experience, company, clients, or anything that has anything to do with what you both do for a living. See the next chapter with an example of 10 non-client interactions.

___ These 10 non-client interactions should be with the CPA that landed your client (or prospect).

___ Continue with the principles with that 1 CPA until you get a referral from the CPA. You will. Stay with it. *Don't give up.*

___ Refer 3 more clients (or prospects) to the CPA. Ideally, you want to wait until you get 1 client referred to you by the CPA, but if you have reached around the 120 day mark with this one CPA, it is time to do this. I will note that if you have not received a referral, you must not be following up consistently or staying in front of the CPA enough. By now you should have had 20 or more interactions with the CPA between interacting with the CPA on your referral and the non-client interactions. I only state this to say, go back and figure out what principles you are breaking, and start again with the CPA from the point you mis-stepped. *You need to override that.*

Why am I now referring 3 clients? I only go 1 client referred to me? Or worse, I haven't received a referral yet.

You are referring 3 clients (or prospects) to go ***all in!***

If you are working with the 1 client you referred, moving forward with 10 non-client interactions (see next chapter), and you refer 3 more clients, you will be in major, consistent contact with this 1 CPA.

The CPA doesn't have to land all 3.

I will repeat here that you MUST follow the principles I laid out on how to refer.

No, you are <u>not</u> referring all 3 clients (or prospects) *at the same time.* Spread it out over 6 weeks; 1 every other week.

Start the process with the first of these three referrals like you had before. *Don't assume anything.* Go back to the beginning of the process of interacting with the CPA with a client. And you will start the same process the same with the second and third referral.

This is allowing you to now increase the interaction with the CPA on multiple levels with multiple clients. At some point in this process you are going to get a referral from the CPA.

__ Interact with the CPA's referral 20 times. Not 20 times with the CPA. 20 times *with the client*. Include the CPA according to my principles. Include non-business interactions with the client referred, including hand-written notes, etc. *This is your ONE shot to impress the CPA, by landing that ONE client referred to you.*

AFTER 6 MONTHS

__ Interact with this one special CPA at least 30 times annually, with a combination of non-client and client interactions. You should be interacting about every other week. Remember the times NOT to interact.

__ Never stop this.

__ The last person someone talks to, typically is the one they refer to. That needs to be you.

__ Your competition is going to take note of this CPA, and will be trying to move in. *Stay present.*

__ Don't ever let go! And don't screw it up. Follow the 100 Do's and 100 Don'ts, until the CPA tells you otherwise.

10 NON-CLIENT INTERACTIONS

PROVEN EXAMPLE

This should be with the CPA that landed your client (or prospect). This is going to require some minor amount of investment of time and resources. So this needs to be with the one that you feel it will count with. This should go without saying, in all that you do, with the CPA, be sincere. If you can't be sincere, the CPA will know it. You cannot be salesy. You have to trust the process. Note how carefully I state what to do, and NOT to do, as this is about getting the CPA to trust you, *and your motives.*

I am not going to keep stating, follow my principles, but with everything, follow my principles.

Here is an example of non-client interactions and how you can successfully accomplish 10 non-client interactions that build on one another:

1. Hand-written note of thanks for taking time with you after you have visited by phone or in person, for the first time. NOTHING MORE STATED THAN THIS. *"Jim, Just a note of thanks for your time. – JJ"* NOTHING MORE! AND DO <u>NOT</u> INCLUDE YOUR BUSINESS CARD. THAT SIMPLE!

2. Break bread with the CPA, so to speak. And buy! Having something to eat or drink with someone creates a completely different bond, even for the shortest amount of time.

3. Hand-written note of thanks for having coffee/breakfast/lunch/dinner/drinks with me. NO I AM NOT KIDDING! You are writing <u>another</u>

hand-written note. NO BUSINESS CARD. You are going to simply state, *"Jim, Thank you for having coffee/breakfast/lunch/dinner/drinks with me! -JJ"* That is it! Nothing more! Nothing!

4. By now you should know something personal about the CPA. Where they went to school, their favorite sport or team; something! **_Mail_** a gift that is less than $25 (before postage) that is of that school, team, sport. Not a joke, prank, dumb gift. Something classy, small that they will PUT IN THEIR OFFICE, and be constantly reminded of you! That they may possibly tell someone about YOU, when that someone asks about what's in their office. *Follow!?*

5. Three days after the gift arrives, email the CPA, and simply state, *"Jim, I hope you don't mind, I mailed you're a gift. Just wanted to make sure you got it. –*

JJ" NOTHING MORE. Don't bring up the client or ask for a meeting or inquire of anything about anything other than the gift you sent. What will be even more golden is if the CPA beats you to the punch and sends you a "thank you!" That counts as the 5th interaction, big time! You are waiting 3 days; in case the CPA wrote you a note of thanks and time for the CPA to open it.

6. Have someone besides you (your assistant) drop by donuts on a Friday morning, having them delivered the moment they open. On the inside of the lid (not on top), write nothing more than this, *"Appreciate you all! – JJ"* You are writing it on the inside so that when the donut box is open, which will be most of the time it sits in the lunch-room, everyone will see your name. *And guess what?* If they don't know who you are, they will ask someone in that office.

"Who is JJ?" And it most likely it will be something positive about you. This also allows you to show your support, respect and true appreciation for the CPA's team.

7. <u>Email</u> the CPA and offer them 2 tickets to something in town that requires tickets, THAT YOU ARE NOT ATTENDING. You are emailing them so as to *not* put the CPA on the spot. Can be anything! Well, maybe avoid a death-metal rock concert (unless the CPA likes that), praise & worship concert (unless the CPA told you what religion they are and this particular event they told you they want to go to) or a political fundraiser. It needs to be some kind of *entertainment that is neutral.* IT DOES NOT MATTER IF YOU DO NOT KNOW IF THE CPA likes baseball, basketball, ballet, etc. It is the gesture. You are

giving them something that is an event, that they can share with someone else, besides you. DO NOT INVITE A CPA TO AN EVENT _WITH YOU_ THAT REQUIRES TICKETS unless it is back-stage with your favorite band AND THEIRS. You cannot get this personal with the CPA at this point. It won't work to be spending this much personal time _with_ the CPA. You want to give them something that they can (and most likely will) accept, and IF THEY DON'T LIKE IT, they can give those tickets to someone else, such as one of their family members or staff. These don't need to be front row, but not nose bleeds, seats.

8. Mail them an article you came across that has something to do with something else they like personally, different from what ever it was with your gift. If you send a gift with LA Dodgers on it, and

later an article about the LA Dodgers, it will feel like the same thing. You want it to be personal, and different to show the CPA you are paying attention to them, personally. Again, NOTHING to do with work, their profession, your services or products, a competitor of theirs or yours. And when you send the article, do NOT fold it. Send it in a 9 x 12 envelope, hand-addressed to the CPA. Have a simple sticky note on it (your company logo on it is fine) that simply says, *"Jim, thought you might enjoy reading this. – JJ"*

9. Break bread with the CPA again. Buy! But hope they buy! Let them buy if they offer. The second instance of breaking bread with someone is going to lead to great communication, especially when you do everything you can to NOT bring up work. Talk about the gift you sent, the tickets you gave, the

article you sent. And I don't mean like a goof. Tell them the story how you came across the gift, the tickets, or the article. This easily reminds the CPA of all the past interactions by just telling them about it.

10. Send them another hand-written note, that simply says, *"Jim, So great to see you again! I appreciate your time. -JJ"*

Continue with the principles with that 1 CPA until you get a referral from this CPA.

You will.

Stay with it.

Don't give up.

YOU WILL CRACK THE CPA CODE

So that's it. *Pretty easy, right?*

I will tell you this. You do all this. You stick to these principles. You don't give up on the process. You stay. You work on it. You will, I promise, find that 1 CPA that will unlock all your dreams my friend!

CPAs are the most loyal professional you will ever come across. And once you prove yourself to the CPA, you will have found someone you can trust with your clients. It will become less about the financial success and more about taking care of the client. Which in turn, will only lead to more success.

Ready to actually start? Easy. Make a list of 30 CPAs and…

One last thing.

I tell everyone, YOU'VE NEVER MET A CPA, QUITE LIKE ME, and the truth of it is, *you've never met a CPA quite like the one you are getting ready to do business with!*

I offer workshops on this. Check out my website for more details. **www.jjthecpa.com**

THANK YOU SO MUCH FOR BUYING AND READING MY BOOK! *I APPRECIATE YOU!*